DIVINE SPARK

The Case for

Spiritual intelligence (SI)

(3rd edition)

Frank MacHovec PhD

The most beautiful emotion we can experience is the whole power of all true art and science. To whom this emotion is a stranger, who can no longer wonder and stand rapt in awe is as good as dead. To know that what is impenetrable to us really exists, manifesting itself as the highest wisdom and the most radiant beauty which our dull faculties can comprehend only in primitive form, this knowledge, this feeling is at the center of true religiousness. In this sense I belong to the ranks of the devoutly religious.

-- Albert Einstein

ACKNOWLEDGMENTS

Every effort was made to credit all sources, cited in the text and/or references after the last chapter. Most quotes were taken from source material or standard references such as *Bartlett's familiar quotations* (Beck, 1968), Frank's *Quotationary* (1999), and Leaven (1955). If there is anything not cited it was used in good faith and according to fair use.

FOREWORD

Religious extremism in the Middle East has disrupted world peace as it did 1000 years ago in the Crusades. It is as if the human race doesn't learn from experience. Prejudice hurts. Distortion and delusion kill. Sadly, it can happen anywhere. U. S. abortion clinic physicians have been shot. Violence between Arab and Israeli in Jerusalem, Hindu and Muslim in the Kashmir, and Catholic and Protestant in Northern Ireland are power struggles rooted in religious differences.

As nuclear weapons become more available, the risk of more horrible wars increases. It's ironic that the prophecy of the end of the world are in the name of God rhough such a tragic event is more likely driven by misguided minds of nations or religious extremists. There is hard evidence for that. What a twist of moral judgment, what mental gymnastics, to kill men, women, and children in the name of God. For the rest of us without such extreme views, it is as Thomas Paine observed in 1776: "These are the times that try men's souls."

Thomas Paine also wrote: "Tyranny, like Hell, is not easily overthrown, but we have this consolation with us, that the harder the conflict, the more glorious the final triumph." Triumph in terms of spirituality is within one's self. Shared with others, it becomes an enriched setting for more spiritual growth. In it there is peace, not war, love, not hate. Confucius suggested it 2500 years ago when he observed that peace within one's self and shared with family spreads to the community, nation, and the world.

It is hoped this book provides more light than heat and adds to the positive force the world needs as selfish belief systems move it toward violence. This book does not advocate any religion and recognizes positive and negative aspects openly and objectively. It explores the concept of spiritual intelligence (SI) that is in religion but that is in everyone, the devout, the agnostic, even the atheist.

SI can be the key to world peace and a bridge between religion and science and religion. Research on the Dead Sea Scrolls has proved that scientists and theologians can collaborate to their mutual advantage. SI and religion are related, both searching for truth. SI and science are also related, since SI is a kind of intelligence. It is an inherited genetic trait in everyone and while it may not be possible to increase it, it can be optimized. There is an evolutionary aspect to it. Great thinkers in the golden age of Greece did not produce guns or airliners though they understood the principles involved. They were not ready. As time passed, perception and intelligence increased. We may be more ready for a higher spiritual consciousness today.

I see myself as a simplifier, not a complicater. I see no need to nitpick into details, a bad habit of science, "losing the baby with the bath water." I'm more a lumper than a splitter.

A sincere apology if anything in this book offends you. The intent was not to weaken anyone's faith, but to help realize a higher consciousness. Buddha asked followers to always approach others saying: "This I know. Accept it or reject it. Either way, go in peace." That is also my message to you.

-- The author

CONTENTS

1

DIVINE SPARK?

Michelangelo's vision

> We are the link between
> God and Nature. As
> God descends into us,
> we must ascend to God.
> -- Jili (14th C. Sufi)

Moses, Buddha, Jesus, and Muhammad shaped world religions and world history. While each of them created a different religious tradition, did they have anything in common? To say they were divinely inspired doesn't really answer the question. Critics suggest other motives, from political ambition and the quest for power to mental illness. Much has been written about them, reflecting a wide spectrum of opinion. Mel Gibson's 2004 movie *Passion of the Christ* is the latest mass media production on a religious theme. There have been many, dating back to Cecil B. DeMille's *Ten Commandments* in 1923 and *King of Kings* in 1927.

Painted high on the ceiling of Rome's Sistine Chapel is Michelangelo's *Creation of Adam*. God sits calmly, a hand raised and a finger pointing toward Adam. Adam receives the divine spark of creation with uplifted hand. Their fingers do not touch. It is as if a divine spark passes across a gap between God and humanity. The energy is induced and not direct. That imagery inspired this book's title and its subject. A divine spark is a simple way to describe a truth beyond words. A picture *is* worth a thousand words.

"Divine sparks" occur today as they have since the beginning of time, in great art, music, literature, and the wonders of science and technology. Moses, Buddha, Jesus, Muhammad and other religious figures have received then generated divine sparks of their own. It was a special kind of intelligence, rich in spirituality: spiritual intelligence (SI). Each had a high level of SI, though they differed in how they expressed and used it. As this chapter will show, their achievements are not better explained by other alternatives. SI relates to religion but it is also evident in the arts and sciences. This book samples those sources as it describes spiritual intelligence. Reading and reflecting on this material may trigger a divine spark in you!

Where did the idea of different intelligences begin? In 1993, Harvard psychologist Howard Gardner proposed it in his book *Frames of mind*. He listed seven but suggested there may be more:

Linguistic, in gifted writers, speakers, teachers, politicians

Logic-math, in scientists and mathematicians

Visual-spatial, in architects, artists, pilots, helmsmen, drivers

Musical, in composers, performers

Body-kinesthetic, in athletes, dancers, surgeons

Intrapersonal, in writers, poets, philosophers

Interpersonal, in therapists, salesmen, politicians

Gardner later suggested three others: *naturalist* as in the works of Darwin, Mendel, Muir, *existentialist* in the works of Camus, Sartre, and Heidegger, and *spiritual*, the subject of this book. But, in a 2000 journal article Gardner called SI "problematic" and considered it as an aspect of existential intelligence "that captures at least in part what individuals mean when they speak of spiritual concerns." He conceded that "spirituality is worthy of study as an intelligence if that lens illuminates its nature." It does!

Before Gardner, intelligence was really "school smarts." IQ (mental age divided by physical age then multiplied by 100) is used mainly to place students in classes suited to their mental age. It is scholastic aptitude and predicts success in school. Over time and with more research school smarts became traditional intelligence. It's an example of how a narrow focus can become a standard.

Today's intelligence theory began with Spearman's "g factor," meaning generalized intelligence. In France, Alfred Binet used a standardized test of the mental age of school children. At Stanford, Terman formulated IQ, the intelligence quotient of mental age over physical age x 100. Wechsler created a series of tests that became the U.S. standard. Still widely used, they measure full scale (FSI) intelligence that combines verbal (VIQ) and performance (PIQ) intelligences.

Psychology is slow to accept multiple intelligences. Gardner's retreat from SI may be due to overzealous educators and clergy who applied SI before it was more clearly defined. In a 2000 journal article he complained: "I cannot enumerate how often I have been said to posit a spiritual intelligence though I have never done so and have in fact explicitly rejected that possibility both orally and in writing."

Gardner added: "Intelligence is currently connected to forms of information processing." That is true for traditional intelligence theory, but the key word is *currently*. George Washington might have lived longer if physicians had not bled him on his deathbed. That was the *current* standard! Gardner commented he was "leery of stretching the term intelligence" and feared it would "sacrifice its primary ties with cognition." Isn't that theoretical bias? Scientific objectivity?

Multiple intelligences are evident in achievements beyond education, training, or experience. SI thinking and feeling are distinctive. Unlike other types, there is an expanded, transcending consciousness that differs from that in other intelligence types. Moses, Buddha, Jesus, and Muhammad are examples. What people with a high level of SI think and do has a distinct spiritual quality. "By their fruits you will know them" (*Matthew* 8:16).

Experts have debated whether intelligence can be increased. Arthur Jensen argued it can't. Robert Sternberg cited programs that show it can. Parents, teachers, school, and good material can optimize "native intelligence" and increases in test scores have proved it. A third idea is that intelligence is slowly evolving upward over time, reflected in gradual increases in IQ test scores over decades of time.

The current definition of psychology is that it is *the science of behavior and mental processes.* To limit intelligence only to information processing ignores other mental processes. Spirituality is more than thinking (cognition) or information processing. Many features are mental processes difficult to observe or test. SI doesn't fit the current cognitive bias of current psychology.

Michelangelo, Mozart, and Shakespeare were intelligent. That's obvious in what they produced. They did more than learn a skill and think about it. They mastered their work, surpassed their teachers, and created masterpieces from their own unique vision. Traditional intelligence doesn't explain that higher, gifted level of achievement. Neither does it explain the strong spiritual quality and impact of great works of art, music, and literature. SI is in the difference between art, music, and literature and what sparks a spiritual high. It is in the difference between what is good and what sparks a "spiritual high."

SI can be difficult to understand and may even seem mysterious. Albert Einstein said that "the most beautiful thing we can experience is the mysterious. It is the source of all true art and science." Science doesn't like mysteries. It insists on fact. But, much of what makes life worth living involves more feeling than fact. Science doesn't explain love very well. It knows more about sex than love. Science is more head than heart. Some of life's realities are not so easily proved by today's "head tripping" science. The scope of a mental process can be narrowed just by naming, defining, or reducing it to numbers. Science can sterilize as it cleans and "lose the baby with the bath water." SI can be sanitized to death.

Having high SI and being religious are not at all the same. An atheist can be spiritual but not religious, and a devout churchgoer may be religious but without a high SI level. It's because religion is mainly social, involved in shared group services and activities. SI is personal. It is a specific type of intelligence and a genetic gift. We all have SI but at different levels. Religion can kill, as 9/11 proved, but SI is positive and without violent potential. Its energy flows much like that of love. Religious extremism is spiritual ignorance. There is no SI in it.

What is it like to receive a divine spark? It can be in an instant "Ahah!" that "takes your breath away" or in a slow flow calm reverie or calm reflection. It can be triggered by actions like a word, a touch, a kiss, or by a feeling or thought. It radiates in great art, music, and literature. Oscar-winning composer Elmer Bernstein wrote music for 200 movies. Asked how he did could do that he said: "Sometimes melodies come from playing around on the piano. Sometimes I awaken with one in my head. Sometimes they just come like a miracle from God." Music that stops you and brings tears to your eyes, or a spiritual high is evidence of SI.

Michelangelo chose to depict Adam as an adult. He gave him an adult mind and body. That meant he was mature enough to receive and use divine sparks. We, the human species, are also able to receive and use that divine energy. The German mystic Meister Eckhart referred to "a spark of divine light, a ray of divinity."

In the West, saints, artists, and writers have received flashes of spiritual light. In the East, meditation lights the way to a higher consciousness. SI has evolved from cave drawings through tribal religions to a universal and non-sectarian spirituality. We've come a long way since living in caves. We are more intelligent. As symbolized in Michelangelo's painting on the Sistine Chapel ceiling, God's hand is raised to us. In a non-sectarian context, the positive SI force in the universe is open to us.

A goal of this book is to explore that higher energy and increase its flow to you. You can't receive a divine spark unless your spiritual hand is raised and ready to receive it. Teachers speak of reading readiness. There is spiritual readiness as well. To be spiritually ready you must build an internal SI satellite dish. You need a Zen "third eye" and "third ear." Being ready is like having an inner spiritual battery. Reflecting on ideas such as those in this book can increase the flow of energy into it. As the spiritual battery charges, SI is optimized and the spark gap between you and the highest power in the universe narrows.

EXERCISE 1. *Pause now and check your readiness and openness to continue. Can you relax where you are and read on as if we are in conversation, without pre-judging or bias? Some people hear only what they want to hear. Some hear only part of what is said. There is no intent to convert or weaken whatever faith you have.*

THE FACES OF GOD

Mention spiritual consciousness and most people think of religion. Religion is a belief system, usually in a sect. Spirituality is the most distinctive feature of SI. Religion is not essential to it. SI seeks to develop a higher consciousness. Part of that is a search for life's meaning and one's role in it. That leads to reflecting on what is beyond life.

Is God the highest power in the universe? The traditional concept is that of a wise old man with a big book of everyone's conduct. It is much more than that and greater than any 3-letter word can contain. Zen Buddhism and Taoism consider it too big an idea for words. On the other hand, Buddha didn't feel a God concept is necessary to develop character.

Religious extremists kill in the name of the same God of their victims. Their image of God differs. The terrorist God is vengeful and condones violence. The God of Islam's Qu'ran forbids murder and suicide. Pro-life Christian extremists have killed Christian clinic doctors. The Ten Commandments forbid it. World War 1 German army belt buckles were inscribed: "Gott mit Uns" (God is with us). Japanese in World War 2 believed the Emperor was "the Son of Heaven." Christian and Muslim warriors in the Crusades killed each other in the name of God. The higher consciousness of SI is non-violent. It seeks unity with the higher power regardless of what It is named.

In the East, ideas of creation and creator are more cosmic and less personal. In China's *Book of Tao* (c. 500 BCE): "There is something mysterious, without beginning, without end that existed before the heavens and the earth, everywhere and inexhaustible. I do not know its name, but if I must name it, I call it Tao and hail it as supreme" (Sutra 25). And: "The Tao described in words is not the real Tao. Words cannot describe it. It is the unnamed source of creation. Named, it is the Great Mother of everything" (Sutra 1).

In his *Philosophical Dictionary* (1764) Voltaire described the God of ancient Greece as "a circle the center of which is everywhere and its circumference is nowhere." The *Bhagavad-Gita*, one of India's oldest scriptures, describes the highest power as "the Mighty One." It describes its enormity: "if the radiance of 1000 suns burst forth at once, that would be the splendor of the Mighty One" (2, 11-12).

How can we be so sure God or the highest power is male? Could "It" be female? Or perhaps both, like a Picasso painting? Women give birth, nurse, and care for the newborn. Mother is the first teacher. We speak of Mother Nature and the ancients spoke of Earth Mother. Here's a joke about this idea. Two white racist men were killed in an auto accident. They found themselves in the waiting room of heaven. St. Peter greeted them and told them God would see them one at a time. The first man entered but returned red-faced and said: "No sense you goin' in there. She's colored." God or the highest power source is a very big idea, a cosmic concept we treat too simplistically.

There has been female imagery of higher powers since ancient times. An idol often found in Greece is that of Artemis, a mother figure with many breasts. There is a life-sized statue of her in the Vatican Museum. Another female deity is the Greek Athena. Legend has it Poseidon chose the present-day Acropolis for his temple. Athena also wanted it so, unable to agree, they fought for it. Poseidon lost and founded his temple farther down the coast. The ruins can be seen there. The Oracle of Delphi was a powerful female figure in ancient Greece. She was real, living, and always an older woman. Vestal virgins in ancient Rome enjoyed high status and power. In Egypt, priestesses of Isis had similar high status. How can we be so sure God is a man?

Gender-free names have been used for higher powers, such as the absolute, ultimate, the One, Mystic Unity, and Nature. The Yab-Yum of Tibet is bisexual, shown in equal male and female profile. India's *Legend of Gilgamesh* tells how Sky Father and Earth Mother join in fond embrace where sea and sky meet. Clouds are the product of their love, bringing rain to Earth Mother to sustain life. China's yin-yang symbol shows the balance of forces in nature as two equal but opposite color fields that interact in an S-curve circle.

There is male imagery because society has been male dominated. Examples: God, Allah, Amon, Brahman, Jehovah, and others. God's personality varies with the religion that describes it. We believe what we were taught or what we choose to believe. The total reality of the universe is beyond our current knowledge. There is more to a rose than its name. The same is true for you. There's more to you than your name. There is more SI in you and others than you may know.

Our image of God or the highest power developed over time, from the power of nature and many gods and goddesses to one person. This progression has been slow and for every step forward we seem to take one to the side. The God of Jews and Muslims seems to be more committed to justice. The Christian God seems more forgiving. In the East the focus is not as narrow. Buddha chose building character as more important. World religion is a Whitman's sampler of different ideas.

EXERCISE 2. *What is your conception of God? Where did you get it – from parents, a religion, reading, or your own thought and reflection? Is it more "learned fact" than "felt spiritually?*

REALIZING SI

Religious extremism blocks SI. They are really polar opposites. Religious extremism has led to wars throughout history. 9/11 is but one recent example. Bias, hate, and violence widen the divine spark gap. Believe only you have truth and the gap widens more. The spark can no longer flash across the gap. That is true for religion and for science, in your family and mine, in you and in me. The tragedy of our time is that so few people and nations work to narrow the spark gap and so many widen it. In order to optimize SI, it is necessary to be open to truth from any source. Partial truth is incomplete and the truth is sacred regardless of its source. Your SI readiness can be tested by answering two questions:

1. Have you been open to what you've read so far?

2. Have you received any spiritual light from it?

The divine spark gap narrows with quiet reflection, what is uplifting in nature or art, music, and literature. It narrows when meeting and sharing with others on spiritual high ground. As Alexander Pope put it: "All nature is but art unknown to you; all chance, direction you can't see, all discord harmony not under-stood, all partial evil universal good; and despite pride and erring, one truth is clear: Whatever is, is right."

Religion is supportive in times of need. That support was needed to explore new lands and found colonies. The down side has been slavery, exploitation, witch hunts and discrimination. In a way, we are our own worst enemy when we follow narrow beliefs that exclude or victimize. William Shakespeare aptly observed: "Man, proud man, dressed in a little brief authority, most ignorant of what he's most assured, his glassy essence like an angry ape, plays such fantastic games before high heaven as make the angels weep" (*Measure for Measure*).

Developing SI can be a lonely task because it is personal and not easily shared. It's a process in which you may feel like a child, alone and afraid of the dark, the unknown. Being divine, the spark is always positive. Aristotle knew it 2000 years ago when he reflected: "There is a region of purity, eternity, and changelessness where the spirit enters unhindered, no longer wandering in error but beholding the true and divine." We are all able to be

Adam, hand raised, ready to receive the divine spark of spiritual intelligence.

SI is a genetic gift to everyone. It was known to ancient peoples, though not as a type of intelligence. It may be what has been called enlightenment, grace, or inspiration. They are unique features of SI.

SI AS ENLIGHTENMENT

Light and enlightenment have been used worldwide for centuries to describe spirituality. In the *Old Testament* creation begins with God's command: "Let there be light" (*Genesis*). In *Psalm 119*: "Your word is a lamp to light my path without which I would grope in the darkness." In the *New Testament,* Jesus is quoted as saying: "You are the light of the world" (*Matthew* 5:14). In the *Qu'ran* (35-42) it is said: "God is the light ... like a lamp set in glass in a niche shining like a star" (35-42). Buddha is called "the enlightened one." Socrates spoke of following his "inner lights."

In his *Study of History*, Arnold Toynbee referred to those who sought spiritual light in seclusion: Buddha under the Bodhi tree, Jesus in the desert, Muhammad and Moses at the mountain. Toynbee saw their search as a 2-step process: (1) they isolated themselves so they could learn, reflect, and absorb without distraction. Then (2) when they felt they were ready they returned to share their light with others.

Behavior changes during times of enlightenment. The change can be sudden, as if the divine spark is a shock of new awareness. The Bible story of Saul (St. Paul) on the road to Damascus in *Acts* 9:1-19 is an example. He voiced "murderous threats" against Christians. "A light from heaven flashed" and threw him from his horse. "For three days he was blind and did not eat or drink." Nearby, Ananias had a vision of Saul chosen to "teach Gentiles, their kings, and people of Israel." When Ananias told Saul that his vision returned he was baptized and "began to preach in the synagogues."

Many writers have described the search for light as one of confusion and paradox. Carl Jung wrote: "Yahweh is just and unjust, kindly and cruel, truthful and deceitful." In *Table talk*, Samuel Taylor Coleridge observed "there is much beast and some devil in man; so also there is some angel and some God." In 1776 Tom Paine wrote in *Age of reason*: "One step above the sublime makes the ridiculous, and one step above the ridiculous makes the sublime again." And Tom Stoppard saw "every exit an entrance also" (*Rosencrantz and Gildenstern*). Louis Lamour wisely advised: "There will come a time you believe everything is finished. That will be the beginning" (*Lonely on the mountain*).

Evil has been described as the dark side of human nature. In ancient Persia life was seen as a struggle between forces of light and darkness. The *Dead Sea Scrolls* used similar imagery. Hindu Shiva creates and destroys in a dance of life and death, the drum of life in one hand, a consuming fire in the other. Some wrote of the wish that goodness prevail over evil or light over darkness. In 1762 Jean Jacques Rousseau wrote: "Everything is good when it leaves the hands of the Creator. Nature never deceives us. We deceive ourselves." In a letter to a friend, Albert Einstein wrote: "God is subtle but not malicious. He doesn't play dice with the universe."

SI AS GRACE

Grace is a word with many meanings. We say: "There but for the grace of God go I" and "having grace under fire." Dictionaries define grace as "an elegant manner or movement, a show of good will, or a helpful delay" (a *grace* period). "Saying grace" at meals asks a blessing on food and those who eat it. Religions teach grace is a gift and not a reward. In *Ephesians* 2:8-9 Paul wrote: "Grace is not your doing but a gift from God." He called it "the fruit of the spirit" in his epistles to the Galatians and Romans.

Grace is described as *amazing* in the hymn *Amazing Grace*. Its text: "Amazing grace, how sweet the sound that saved a wretch like me. I once was lost but now am found, was blind and now I see." Blaise Pascal wrote of its power: "By grace we are made like unto God and without it we are like unto brute beasts." In his book *Light of Asia* Edwin Arnold saw Buddha's influence as due to the power of grace: "In many lands and many tongues Buddha gave Asia light, conquering the world with a spirit of strong grace."

In 1991 the World Council of Churches published *Confessing the one faith* to foster a spirit of unity among Christian sects. In it is stated: "The life of the Christian is necessarily one of continuing struggle yet also the continuing experience of grace." Christian religion defines grace in three forms: a favor, a power, or kind of love. Michelangelo showed all three in *Creation of Adam* on the Sistine Chapel ceiling. God is depicted extending a hand, a finger pointing to Adam, to us, humanity at large.

The life of a British sea captain is an example of the power of grace. The son of a sea captain, John Newton's mother died when he was young, and his father took him to sea. At 19 he was impressed on a British warship. He deserted, was caught, flogged, and demoted. He then transferred to a slave ship but was captured by a slave trader. Rescued, he chose to become master of a slave ship. On one voyage there was a terrible storm and the ship was in danger of sinking. Though not religious, he prayed, and the storm passed. He called it his "great deliverance" and celebrated it every year for the rest of his life. From that time on he used his time at sea to improve himself. He married at age 30 and left the sea, never to return.

Newton was ordained and ministered to a small church where he met the poet William Cowper. They became close friends and composed hymns, almost one a week. There were 348 hymns in the 1779 *Olney Hymns*. Among them was *Amazing Grace*, still popular today. It describes the grace Newton felt in the storm: "'Twas grace that taught my heart to fear and grace my fears relieved."

Cowper also wrote about the power of grace. He was troubled most of his life by depression, at times of suicidal depth. As Newton used time at sea to educate himself, Cowper used it to overcome his mental problems. He translated Homer. Cowper and Newton shared their insight in this excerpt:

God moves in a mysterious way his wonders
to perform. He plants his footsteps in the sea
and rides upon the storm. Behind a frowning
providence he hides a smiling face and happiness
depends as Nature shows, less on exterior things
than most suppose.

SI AS INSPIRATION

Writers have described spirituality as an uplifting or god-like feeling of inspiration. In *Perennial Philosophy* Aldous Huxley wrote: "Only becoming Godlike can we know God" by contact with "the divine element, our essential nature." In *Man is not alone*, Abraham Henschel wrote that it is "as if a divine cunning operated using our instincts as pretexts" toward "universally valid goals to harness man's lower forces in the service of higher ends."

In *The old wise man*, Carl Jung wrote: "I cannot say I believe. I know. I have had the experience of being gripped by something stronger than myself, something people call God." Divine sparks of inspiration are within reach in everyday life. They can be calming like the stillness after a storm or the awe in a sunset or sunrise. Saul Bellow described the calming effect of art in George Plimpton's *Writers at work*: "Art has something to do with the achievement of stillness in the midst of chaos. There is a stillness that characterizes prayer, too, and the eye of the storm, an arrest of attention in the midst of distraction."

Divine sparks can be random, spontaneous, such as in suddenly coming upon a sleeping baby. Children, the "puppy people," can be SI spark generators, evoking a warm smile even from strangers. Composers and concert musicians, artists and writers, are also spark generators. There are divine sparks in hunches of scientists. Einstein told his students: "Never lose a holy curiosity."

SI AS INTELLIGENCE

Spiritual intelligence (SI) best explains the spiritual consciousness that formed religions and inspired great works in the arts and humanities. No other intelligence is as good a fit. SI includes grace, enlightenment, inspiration, and many other qualities. It is a universal personality trait and not religious per se though religions reflect it to a greater or lesser extent. The plays of Sophocles survived the test of time for more than 2000 years, evidence of a meaningful message to remain so popular. Freud chose Sophocles' *Oedipus Rex* as a model for father-son rivalry in his Oedipus complex. *Antigone* is a model of high spiritual awareness and moral maturity.

In *Antigone,* King Creon decreed that anyone killed attacking the city would "lay in the field, a sweet treasure for predatory animals and birds." Antigone's brother died attacking the city and was left unburied. She buried him, was arrested, and brought before the king. She admitted "violating the king's law" but said she "followed the immortal unwritten law, not just now but now and forever, beyond man." Creon had her buried alive and from that day all went wrong as if the gods were angry.

There is a divine spark in this story. It is a lesson of love that transcends law. Studies show women are more sensitive than men to this level of awareness. They tend to be more accepting, cooperative, and interdependent. Being relational is the words most used to describe this trait. Men tend to be loners, more independent. Yes, they do tend not to ask directions! Sophocles knew all this 2000 years ago. King Creon behaved with male logic. Antigone was at a higher level. She had higher SI.

Creon's thinking continues today. Might does make what passes for right. Creon is alive and well where there is bias fanned into hate in politics and religion. No nation is free of the dark side. But Antigone also walks the earth. Hers is sadly a small voice in the wilderness. She was there at the *Magna Carta, Mayflower Compact, Declaration of Independence,* and *Gettysburg Address.* In *Les Miserables* she stood with Jean Valjean facing Inspector Jauvert in King Creon's role.

There are SI-sensitive groups in the major religions. They share in the same search for higher truth despite differing beliefs. Examples are Hassidic Jews, Gnostic and Coptic Christians, Sufi Muslims, Zen Buddhists, yogic Hindus, and many New Age sects. The search is not limited to religions. Artists, composers, and writers like Sophocles and Shakespeare are searchers. The West leads the East in science and technology but not in SI. The East has been more open to a free personal search for higher spiritual consciousness.

EXERCISE 3. *Which aspects of spiritual intelligence you've just read seem most valid to you? Is it possible they're all true? Is it possible none of them are true? What does it mean to you?*

<u>YOUR</u> SPIRITUAL AWARENESS

Here's a questionnaire that helps detect spiritual awareness. It does not measure the level of SI but detects its presence. There is no "passing" grade but a score of 50 or more suggests a significant level of spiritual awareness. It is based on a group of clergy and seminary students against a control group of non-clergy volunteers. To take it, respond to each statement using this 5-point scale: a little (0-1); some (2-3); very much (4-5):

1. I have feelings of deep inner peace and a quieter mind in a beautiful garden

2. For me, animals and birds have a spiritual quality.

3. I feel especially moved when I read something that to me is inspirational.

4. I sometimes lose track of time when I see an especially beautiful sunrise or sunset.

5. I can sit alone and have feelings of deep inner peace regardless of what is happening around me.

6. All in all, for me the world is a special sacred place.

7. I have feelings of deep inner peace from music that is restful or inspiring.

8. I sometimes feel connected to a higher consciousness outside myself.

9. All men and women are brothers and sisters in a spiritual sense.

10. Doing good, thinking positively, is as spiritual as it is moral and social.

11. For me, to be happy and content with what I have is a special blessing.

12. A baby is a special spiritual gift to everyone.

13. Art, music, and inspirational reading can be special links to a higher consciousness.

14. There is something spiritual in everything and everyone.

15. Rituals done well have spiritual energy and purpose.

16. Inspiring thoughts and experiences are mostly spiritual for me.

17. Slowing down, stopping to see "with a 3rd eye" in quiet contemplation can be a spiritual experience.

18. Being spiritual is to have the innocence of a baby, the trust of a growing child and the faith of a reflective adult.

19. Spirituality is a link to the universe and beyond.

20. If there is one God, He, She, or It radiates pure spirituality.

From the results and interviews and group discussions following the questionnaire, 16 traits reflecting high SI emerged. They are further explored in Chapter 2.

SPIRITUAL EVOLUTION?

Pierre Teilhard de Chardin was a Jesuit priest and also a paleontologist, an unusual combination. Teilhard (say *Tay-ard*) saw fossil evidence of evolution but as a priest he also believed in a divine origin of creation. His unique contribution was to blend science and religion into a theory of evolving spirituality. It is described in his 1955 book *The phenomenon of man,* first published in France. It became a worldwide best seller.

Teilhard's theory explains how religious thought began with tribal worship and cave drawings and over thousands of years evolved into organized religions. He referred to this process as **hominization** and saw it as developing into an **omega state** of universally shared enlightenment. The down side is the fact that it has been evolving at a very slow rate. Prejudice, persecution, and religious wars have been major obstacles. 9/11 is but a recent example and yet religious extremism continues. Violence in the name of God is a strange paradox but a reality far removed from SI.

No religion has ever become the universal belief system of the world. Jesus was a Jew and Buddha was Hindu but religions they founded went separate ways. There have been schisms in them. Islam, too, split into Sunni and Shi'ite. None of the resulting sects has become the one and only religion of the world. World history suggests it will never happen. But Teilhard's hominization to omega offers the hope that spirituality can overcome these differences, without any loss to sectarian belief. There may yet be Good Samaritans to help humanity realize it potential.

NEGATIVE SI ?

Like other intelligences, SI is a positive trait and potential for higher consciousness. There is no negative SI. If there is a down side to SI it is in not developing it. History proves religious belief can lead to extremism and extremism to violence. Jonathan Swift wrote: "We have enough religion to make us hate but not enough to love one another." No religion has been immune to a self-righteous disregard of the beliefs of others.

The genocide of six million Jews in World War 2 surpassed the deaths in all the religious wars in history. That it happened in the 20th century suggests the human species is not as mature as it would like to believe. Wars and violence that involve religious belief continue, most recently in Kosovo, Northern Ireland, Jerusalem, the Kashmir, Sri Lanka, Africa, and Indonesia to 9/11.

In his 1968 book *Faith and violence*, Thomas Merton described how "popular religion" can lead to "a self-frustrating and self-destroying culture." He wrote:

> The clichés of popular religion have in many cases been every bit as hollow and as false as those of soap salesmen and more dangerously deceptive because one cannot so easily verify the claims made about the product. The sin of religion is it has turned God, peace, happiness, salvation and all that man desires into products to be marketed in a specious attractive package deal (p. 116).

Self-indulgent leaders mislead followers and block SI. Spiritual traits of leaders can be more illusion than real. Hero worship can fog the mind. Merton suggested we may be "the champion idolaters of all history." He wrote: "We are more inclined to idolatry because we imagine we are, of all generations, most enlightened, most objective, most scientific, most progressive, and most humane. This is in fact an image of ourselves that is false and also the object of a cult. We worship ourselves in this image.

Merton wrote that we can lose objectivity "by devout and blind fidelity to myth." He described one such myth: "If the adversary is by definition wicked, then objectivity consists simply in refusing to believe he can possibly be honest in any circumstances whatever." Faced with facts to the contrary a common defense has been to see them as potential evil. Merton wrote: "We determine beforehand we will be swayed by no fact that does not accord perfectly with our own preconceived judgment."

Illusions or delusions of charismatic leaders can block spiritual growth. It is groupthink, not a personal or free search for spiritual light. There may be some meditative awareness but it is likely it is shaped by the group or leader. Our trust in science can limit and shape what we think and believe. Merton asked: "Could science itself be our number one superstition?"(p. 152).

When SI is blocked, baser motives meet less resistance. As dark motives grow they prevent optimizing SI. This helps explain religious extremists. No religion is safe from them. Will-to-power replaces spiritual values. Often it is disguised. Afghan Talibans began as a reform movement to restore law and order after the Russian occupation. It became a theocracy of rigid intolerance, with public beatings and executions at stadium soccer games.

Islam's *Qu'ran* contradicts Muslim extremists: "People of the Book do not go to excess in religion and do not say of God anything but truth (*Women, 171*). The *Qu'ran* forbids religious intolerance: "Be they Muslims, Jews, Christians, or Sabians, those who believe in God, the Last Day, and who do good shall have their reward with their Lord (*Cow, 62*). Extremism is more a political power motive. As such it is of little spiritual value.

There is a downward spiral from personal bias to believing in violence to impose your will on others. We are all biased in one way or another. We have our favorite food, fashion, and friends, politics and religion. They are not extreme nor harmful to others. People with strong opinions advocate for a cause and there is negative potential in doing so. Personal opinion, a bias, can lead to distorted thinking and the "cognitive dissonance" that Leon Festinger found, to delusion. Facts are ignored or twisted. Anger heats to hate, then rage, against a perceived evil. The evil must be stopped at any cost. The misguided become enforcers and martyrs. Terrorism and war, suicide and murder, slavery and persecution become means to the end, the one right way. Delusion becomes truth.

The history of Hawaii is an example of how religion can inadvertently help create a negative effect. There were no wars for 1000 years until Tahitian warriors invaded. They imposed their culture dominated by *mana,* a value system based on power and aggression. Until 1840 there were wars between competing kings until the islands were united by King Kamehameha. The first Europeans arrived in 1778, mainly seafarers, later Christian missionaries.

In time, native Hawaiians became the minority. In 1898 non-native citizens led a revolt to overthrow the government and cede it to the United States. The queen, Liliokalani, was forced to abdicate. Ironically, she wrote many songs, one being *Aloha Oe.* Hawaii calls itself "the Aloha state." Aloha means more than "hello." It also means love.

What happened to Hawaii has been repeated world-wide. Native peoples such as Aztec, Mayan, and Inca in Central and South America, and tribes in the United States suffered the same erosion of traditions and values. China did the same to Tibet. There are many examples. In world history, domination and exploitation are more the norm than freedom and self-determination. In 1945, the United Nations charter recommended territories colonized by other nations be given the choice to continue or become independent. In 1959, Hawaiians were given one choice, to continue as a territory or become a state. Independence was not offered.

The negative effect of domination was acknowledged by President Grover Cleveland in 1893. He called it "a substantial wrong." In 1993, Congress issued a formal apology to Hawaii. In it, Congress conceded that prior to 1778 Hawaii had "a highly organized, self-sufficient, subsistent social system based on communal land tenure and a sophisticated language, culture, and religion" the United States recognized from 1826 to 1893. With a refreshing candor it referred to "the deprivation of the rights of Native Hawaiians to self-determination" by "a small group of non-Hawaiian residents" who "conspired to overthrow the indigenous and lawful Government of Hawaii."

Acknowledging a wrong is a noble first step toward reconciliation. The UN charter added impetus for the independence of third world nations. The Congressional apology reflected an open appreciation of other cultures. These are positive steps toward a more moral and fair world and may some day become the norm. On the down side, the drive to dominate continues. It is evident that wherever guns are used to impose on system over another. The ambition of Hitler and Stalin in World War 2 is one example. It cost the lives of millions. In what seems a psychotic twist, many of the guns firing today are in the name of Allah. The risk of conflict and violence increases when a religion steadfastly claims to be the only source of truth and seeks to impose that truth by force.

EVIL

Evil has been described in all the scriptures of world religions. In *Genesis* Adam and Eve ate the forbidden fruit of the tree of knowledge. Freud might smile and call it evidence of the defense mechanism of denial. Adam blamed Eve. Eve blamed the snake. The snake probably blamed God. The first account of murder in the *Bible* is also in *Genesis,* Abel killing his brother Cain. Those ancient evils involved close relationships of husband and wife and between brothers.

There is power in evil. It moves people to do what is against their moral code. It has been vented in between Catholics and Protestants in Belfast, Jew and Muslim in Jerusalem, Hindu and Muslim in the Kashmir, between Christian and Muslim in Kosovo, Indonesia, and Iraq. Freud saw evil as basic in human nature. He called it the *thanatos libido.* The *eros libido* is its opposite. Henrik Ibsen wrote: "Look into any man's heart and you will always find one black spot which he has to keep concealed."

In the *New Testament* Jesus saw evil as basic to human nature when he said to men about to stone a prostitute: "Let him who is without sin cast the first stone" (*John,* 8:7). King Solomon is quoted as saying: "There is no one who does not sin" (*1 Kings* 8:46). Seeing evil as coming from Satan or a devil lessens personal responsibility: "The devil made me do it." In *Lord* Jim, a story with a theme of good and evil, Joseph Conrad wrote: "The belief in a supernatural source of evil is not necessary. Men alone are quite capable of every wickedness."

An open mind is the gateway through which SI flows. Strong personal opinion renders SI less positive. Obsessing about minor details can lead to distorted thinking. If it is unchecked, distortion can become delusion in a downward spiral into mental illness. Optimizing SI is achieved alone, so there are no safeguards to prevent excess or   errors. Non-SI forces within the personality can lead away from spirituality to distorted thinking and mental illness.

Symptoms of mental disorder can involve religious ideas. Some believe they hear the voice of God or they are Jesus or some other divine person. This is mental illness and not SI. There are many examples: the mass suicide of more than 900 men, women, and children in the *Peoples' Church* in Guyana; David Koresh's refusal to submit to lawful authority in Waco; and Marshall Applewhite's *Heaven's Gate* commune that suicided to enter the Hale-Bopp comet.

It is important to ensure you are on a healthy track to higher SI. The signs are always positive. It is not unusual to withdraw somewhat socially from others, though not completely. There may be some distancing from others but not because of distrust. Some self-talk is normal but hearing voices that command action against others is not. Sleep problems, appetite or weight gain or loss, or lack of interest in the usual pastimes are not signs of optimizing SI.

A mentor or guru can help you stay on track but there is a down side. Some support is helpful but there is some risk of becoming dependent. There is risk, too, of undue influence. Many have been misled. Jim Jones and his Peoples' Church led more than 900 men, women, and children to Guyana where they died in a mass suicide. Followers of Marshall Applewhite in his Heaven's Gate cult shared a similar fate.

The search for spiritual consciousness and the descent into mental illness are both solitary experiences. What seems to be mystic thought can be a sign of mental illness. It is not always easy to see what is right and wrong and choosing between them. Much of life involves choosing between the lesser of several evils.

Johann Faustus was a 16th century mystic and professor. His achievements became legendary. Martin Luther knew of him. After Faustus' death, a rumor spread that he was given special powers by a devil, Mephistopheles. For years of power and pleasure Faustus agreed to be forever damned to hell. It took Johann Wolfgang Goethe many years to write his version of the story (1808 to 1832 CE).

It is said it took that long to decide whether to save or damn Faustus. He chose to save him. It is an interaction of good with evil, ambition, and the wisdom of aging. Goethe, himself aging, gave the aging Faust increasing insight from suffering, and a developing SI.

The world could benefit from a Declaration of Spiritual *Inter*dependence embracing the best in all religions and omitting weaknesses in each. Violence and wars in the name of religion may seem like we are in dark times. Violence is a primitive way to solve problems. It shows the human race hasn't learned enough about tolerance. It suggests religion has not yet helped us to accept each other, especially those who do not believe as we do. In past centuries we felt compelled to overcome them by force or by our faith. We presumed to replace what was there with what we had here. Have we been more Cain than Good Samaritan? Is humanity's glass half full or half empty?

Moses, Buddha, Jesus, and Muhammad generated high SI. They received a divine spark and passed it on. Their lives and works clearly show it. No other type of intelligence better fits what they said and did. The world's great art, music, and literature also generate sparks and

SI. These are all rich sources of evidence for SI that have been ignored by science.

Until Muhammad, great spiritual leaders arrived about every 500 years. There was Moses, then Buddha, LaoTse, and Kung FuTse, then Jesus and Muhammad. We haven't had any others for over a thousand years. That may be because we've reached an SI level high enough to continue on our own without a facilitator. It is as if God or the highest power gave each of us a mind and body and said: "Here, see what you can do with it." If that is so, we have an awesome responsibility and a wonderful opportunity. We can truly become ourselves, realize our potential, and gradually expand consciousness.

In 100 BCE Terence, a Roman senator's freed slave, became a playwright. He suffered enough to see life's glass as half empty yet he wrote: "Where there's life, there's hope." In 1734 Alexander Pope added: "Hope springs eternal." Ernest Hemingway saw war firsthand and in *For whom the bell tolls* he wrote: "The world is a fine place, worth fighting for, and I hate very much to leave it." Perhaps this is what the *Old Testament* psalmist meant: "What is man that you are mindful of him, that you care for him? You made him a little lower than the angels and crowned him with glory and honor. You made him ruler over the works of his hands; you put everything under his feet (8:5)." In his epistle to the Corinthians, Paul expressed a similar thought: "The Lord has assigned to each his task" (I.3:5) and "now we see a poor reflection as in a mirror; then we shall see face to face. Now I know in part; then I shall know fully even as I am fully known" (I.13:11-12).

SI better defines spirituality than the others described here. Enlightenment, grace, and inspiration are aspects of

SI. Like the concept of God there is a lot more to it. SI is a divine spark in people. It's what some call "God in man" when they say God and heaven are here on earth. SI includes spiritual evolution, the human race coming of age spiritually. That process is slowed by violence and wars. SI also better defines spirituality because it applies to everyone, the churched and unchurched, and religions that no longer exist. It is universal and not sectarian. It accepts the spirituality of Buddha, Moses, Jesus, and Muhammad since truth is sacred regardless of its source. In the words of Islam's *Qu'ran* all religions are "people of the book." SI was the same trait in Plato and Plotinus, Aesop and Aristotle, Marcus Aurelius and Maimonides. It is completely non-sectarian.

We live at a time when religious differences continue to be divisive and lead to conflict and violence. We can continue to raise our hand in anger or extend it to others in a good faith search for common ground. Hands across differences are in similar position to Michelangelo's God and Adam. It is the kind of relationship and the conditions when divine sparks occur. It can be so for the peoples of this troubled world.

EXERCISE 4. *Read again the pages on negative SI. Check yourself on each of the negatives described. There should not be any in your journey to higher spiritual awareness. They dim the light of SI.*

SI SPARKS

SI sparks are short quotations with a spark of SI. When Buddha was asked to define truth he said it is like a diamond with many facets, each reflecting an aspect of truth. Absolute truth is the total diamond in all its aspects.

Truth can seem to vary according to how and where it is seen. Sometimes we see only part of the truth. Seeing the whole truth takes work. It's more earned than learned. There are 120 numbered SI sparks in this book and many quotes rich in SI throughout the text. Each sparks some SI light. Reflect on them. Refer back to them from time to time to help develop and expand your SI.

1. Like it or not, know it or not, all nature secretly seeks God, and tries to ferret out the track on which God may be found (Meister Eckhart).
2. Nature is saturated with deity (Ralph Waldo Emerson).
3. What else is Nature but God and Divine Reason that pervades the whole universe and all its parts (Seneca).
4. Visible marks of extraordinary wisdom and power appear so plainly in all the works of creation that a rational person cannot miss discovering deity (John Locke).
5. The universe is a coded message from God (Malcolm Muggeridge).
6. God provides the thread for the work begun (James Howell).
7. I took a day to search for God and found Him not. But as I trod by rocky ledge, through woods untamed, just where one scarlet lily flamed, I saw His footprint in the sod (William Bliss Carman).
8. A certain purification of intelligence can open the spirit to a higher and more illuminating understanding of the meaning and purpose of life or indeed the very nature of being itself (Thomas Merton, *Mystics and Zen masters*).
9. God expects but one thing of you, that you let God be God in you (Meister Eckhart).

10. God lives in the heart of every creature (*Bhagavad Gita,* ca. 6th century BCE).

2

WHAT'S IT LIKE?

The S-traits

> We and God have business
> with each other. Opening
> ourselves to His influence
> fulfills our deepest destiny.
> -- William James (1902)

The scientific method, common to all the sciences, requires that whatever is studied must first be defined. That is needed to ensure everyone understands the subject. Others can then research and refine it. For SI, being an intelligence, a genetic personality trait, puts it in psychology's arena. Everyone is born with it though it varies from one person to another like any of the other type of intelligence.

Like other types of intelligence, SI can be masked in a poor environment or enriched in a more positive setting. Studies have proved intelligence can be optimized in a supportive environment. For SI, the improvement is an increased awareness of one's self as a spiritual being and a higher consciousness. Since SI is a relatively new concept there has been little research on it. It is not yet possible to clearly define it.

Words from science or religion are not adequate. SI differs from faith. As an intelligence, SI is not necessarily religious. Faith is an aspect of religion, based on a belief system. SI is inherited, a gift of nature or nature's God, more caught than taught. Faith is more involved more on doing, SI more on perceiving. Faith is fixed, usually on a moral code. SI is fluid, rising to a higher consciousness. Unlike other types of intelligence, higher consciousness is distinctly spiritual. Faith controls awareness; SI expands it. SI is not supernatural.

S-TRAITS

Abraham Maslow researched normal, well adjusted people. Some were what he called self-actualized. They seemed better adjusted, somehow happier. He found traits in them he named B-values, values of becoming. Using similar methods, traits of people with high SI are evident. Some are similar to Maslow's B-values. That isn't surprising since being self-actualized involves thinking and feeling in ways that reflect high SI. To keep SI traits separate from Maslow's they are called S-traits.

S-traits emerged from the results of the *Spiritual Awareness Inventory* (in Chapter 1) and before-and-after interviews and discussions. There are 16. People with high spiritual awareness tend to have highly developed S-traits. Clergy and seminary students who took the inventory reported higher levels of S-traits than the general public. The 16 S-traits:

1. Meditative awareness
2. Esthetic awareness
3. Moral maturity
4. Character, integrity
5. Empathy
6. Openness
7. Growth drive
8. Selfless service
9. Modesty, humility
10. Compassion, caring

11. Positive attitude
12. Elegant simplicity
13. Spontaneity
14. Honest candor
15. Spiritual introjections
16. Spiritual humor

1. MEDITATIVE AWARENESS

This is a major S-trait and may be the most distinct sign of high SI. Immanuel Kant described what meditative awareness is like in his *Critique of Pure Reason:* "The countless multitude of worlds annihilates my importance on a planet that is a mere speck in the universe but moral law elevates my worth as an intelligence in which moral law reveals to me a life independent of animality and of the whole sensible world, reaching to the infinite. This was known and valued by the ancients."

Meditative awareness was known thousands of years ago. Ptolemy wrote in the first century: "I am mortal but when I see the starry night I am no longer earthbound but join the universe and am immortal with it" (Beck, 1968). At that same time Marcus Aurelius, a pagan, observed: "There is nowhere m ore quiet or free than your own soul. This is especially true when thinking brings deep inner peace, a good state of mind. Find and go to your own peaceful retreat and let simple truths cleanse your soul and relieve you of any discontent" (Leavens, 1955). The 18th century theologian Auguste Sabatier wrote: "the essence of religion is a conscious willful relation of the soul with the mysterious power on which it feels it and its destiny depend" (Beck, 1968). The *Old Testament* sounded a similar chord: "Your old men shall dream dreams, your young men shall see visions" (*Joel* 2:28).

Meditative awareness can be developed anywhere, any place, whatever you're doing. In his 1929 book *The Prophet*, Kahlil Gibran suggested: "Your daily life is your temple and your religion. If you would know God be not a solver of riddles. Look and you will see him playing with your children. Look into space and you will see him walking in the cloud." James Martineau gave this advice:

> Go into silence. Strip yourself of all pretense, selfishness, sensuality, and lethargy. Lift off thought after thought, passion after passion, to reach the inmost depth of all, and how deep its perspective, how ancient its forms of light. Think of how little you know of God and the mysteries of life. It will be strange if you do not feel the Eternal Presence and the astonishment at how small the dust that blinded you from the height of quiet holy love. Imprisoned no more in a small compartment of time, you belong to eternity which is here and now, at one with Heaven you will have found the secret place of the Almighty (Leavens, 1955).

14th century Chinese poet Meng Shu Ching wrote:
> On the low wall of my garden there stands a tiny shrine half hidden in the shadow of the trees. When I am weary of this sad world and man's turmoil and strife I steal off to my shrine among the trees. There, with silent prayer and incense I find my soul again and thank Heaven for my shrine among the trees (Leavens, 1955).

Meditative awareness is a kind of childlike openness, accepting and receptive. Abraham Maslow described it as "a natural ability to contemplate, savor, marvel at, and be fascinated with and hopefully enjoy what is happening or not happening at the time, the way children experience the world intently absorbed, spellbound, popeyed, and enchanted" (1971). In his 1971 book *The occult*, Colin Wilson used this example: "Consciousness is as powerful as a microscope, but another kind of consciousness is needed equivalent to a telescope." He called that mental telescope *Faculty X* and "the paradox is we already possess it to a large degree."

Meditative awareness is at a higher level of perception than the normal awake state. The conscious mind taps direct literal meaning, the surface content of verbatim facts, events, and experiences. For SI, there are three levels: literal or external reality; underlying, such as a moral or greater principle; and meditative, higher truth that transcends the other two. Antigone was at that level when she stood before King Creon, Moses to the pharaoh, and Jesus before Pilate.

Spiritual development in the East and West differ in their use of meditation. Most Western religions do not emphasize it or use it the same way. Eastern religions rely on it as a vital part of "mindfulness." Many studies have confirmed the value of meditation. In one study Jesuit novices were divided into two groups (Sacks, 1979). One group meditated alone for four weeks meditating alone. The other was a control group, not secluded or meditating. Only the meditating group achieved what was referred to as "a unified self system."

Meditative awareness comes by emptying the mind and letting go of whatever was there. In Zen it is said you must empty a cup before it can be filled. A full (not mindful) mind is like a full stomach. Thinking and awareness slows. Russian mystic Gurdjieff described most people as being "asleep" and they resist and resent being awakened. That sleep is the trance-like state of everyday life without meditative awareness. Mindfulness is being fully awake to the moment, like an indifferent observer. In Zen it is "seeing with a third eye and hearing with a third ear."

The mindful state is one of meditative awareness, a spiritual consciousness. In it there is no need to act on what is thought, felt, sensed or perceived. There is no judgment of good or bad, no labeling. Depression or anxiety, two frequent reactions to life stress, are not triggered because they are not acted on (reinforced).

2. ESTHETIC AWARENESS

Those with high SI have, as Maslow reported "an eye for beauty and elegance." They see, hear, and feel the spiritual quality in great art, music, writing, and even from a person, a place or thing, a thought or feeling. Being sensitive to these divine sparks is the S-trait of esthetic awareness. It is the ability to find spiritual value and feel its force beyond the satisfaction of the moment. A sign of it is the "Ahah!"or "goose flesh" moving moment from art, music, literature, a life situation, in something spoken or written.

This S-trait can be further developed by taking time and effort to experience the spiritual nature of life in its many forms. This can be done observing nature and people. There are divine sparks in the sky, its color from time to time, clouds that form and change. This way of catching the spark is to be as free as a child. It is to be an

Eternal Child. Remember imagining what clouds looked like when you were a child?

Without staring, observe people, especially children whose feelings are still pure and natural. Listen more closely to people, what they say and how they say it, their voices and feeling tone. At the end of each day think of what was most esthetically elegant. It could be a rain drop on your face and nothing more. If you can't recall any, imagine what could have happened with esthetic impact. Tune in to the surrounding symphony of nature around you.

3. MATURE MORALITY

Having moral maturity is the ability to steer a course between conformity and non-conformity. Antigone had it. Maslow described it well: "A good-humored rejection of stupidities and imperfections but with a greater or lesser effort at improving them" (1968). Growing up morally begins with "doing the right thing" and continues upward to a more aware level. It accepts societal values but transcends them in a higher consciousness. People with this S-trait grow up. They don't just grow old.

The ecumenical movement reflects this higher level of moral maturity. An example is the 1965 Second Vatican Council's *Nostra Aetate* ("in our time") that deplored blaming Jews for Jesus' crucifixion. Moral maturity is at a level above sectarian conflict. It bridges gaps without lessening the faith of those who differ. Extremism is morally immature.

This S-trait can be developed by applying a moral view of a current event. Choose an editorial, letter-to-the-editor, news item, or someone's public comment as a starting point to envision other views. The subject should be put in total perspective and level of moral maturity. The SI criteria are similar to Lawrence Kohlberg's system, a standard reference in psychology textbooks:

PRE-CONVENTIONAL LEVEL (self-interest)
Stage 1: Punishment-obedience (fear authority; avoid punishment)
Stage 2. Instrumental purpose (eye-for-eye justice)

CONVENTIONAL LEVEL (social approval)
Stage 3: Interpersonal cooperation, approval, affection, Golden Rule)
Stage 4: Maintaining social order (societal values)

POST-CONVENTIONAL LEVEL (abstract ideals)
Stage 5: Social contract (values adapted to laws and rules)
Stage 6: Universal ethical principle (universal values)

Moral truth is universal, not man-made, the same across the long sweep of history, as true now as it was in ancient times, and anywhere in the universe. It is Antigone's higher truth and not King Creon's law, Socrates' inner lights and not the judgment of his jury.

4. CHARACTER, INTEGRITY

There is a distinctly spiritual quality in the personality of people with high SI, evident in what they do and say, their attitude and behavior, even in their tone of voice and choice of words. They seem to be in a state of grace that inspires others. Washington, Jefferson, Lincoln, and Gandhi had it. There is an inner calm, what Buddhists call *equanimity* and described in the *New Testament* as "the peace that transcends all understanding" (*Philippians 4:7*).

People of character and integrity are often described as "knowing who they are" or "being comfortable with themselves." They help others find themselves. Assessing yourself for this S-trait is difficult. "To see ourselves as others see us" as the poet Robert Burns put it, is a rare ability. It's better to rely on others, those close to you and those distant from you. People without any ulterior motive to flatter or criticize are especially helpful. You may have to use a Zen third eye and ear to get the truth.

A *contract partner* is a great help. You "contract" with a trusted person to give you feedback on what you want to change in yourself, an aspect of your personal growth. That's half a contract. Your half is to give the contract partner feedback about something she or he wants or needs.

5. EMPATHY

Carl Rogers felt empathy is essential for anyone who wants to help others. He emphasized the need for "un-conditional positive regard." Empathy is fellow feeling and family feeling in an unbiased respect for others that is real, not "politically correct" or "the thing to do." It is being genderless, ageless, racially color-blind, being moved by the life by the problems of others. It was reflected in Mother Teresa's caring for the needy, Gandhi's compassion for the untouchables, in the Biblical Good Samaritan, and Buddha "the compassionate one."

6. OPENNESS

A sign of this S-trait is being open to truth regardless of its source, to understand truth has many facets, many paths to the same destination. Those with it have what Maslow (1970) called "real receptivity of the Taoistic sort" which he explained further as a "difficult achievement to really listen wholly, passively, and self-effacingly without presupposing, classifying, improving, controverting, evaluating, approving or disapproving, without dueling with what is said, rehearsing the rebuttal in advance, without free-associating to portions of what is being said so that succeeding portions are not heard at all."

Maslow saw children as "abler than their parents to look and listen and to listen in an absorbed way." This is consistent with the *New Testament:* "Unless you become as little children you shall not enter into the kingdom of heaven" (*Matthew* 18:3). Openness is in how well you listen and understand the opinion of others, whether you agree or disagree. It doesn't mean yielding or changing unless you freely choose to do so.

A critic viewing a painting of Jesus standing at a door pointed out there was no door knob. The artist replied it was the door to the heart and can only be opened from inside. Hate, violence, and wars are the acts of closed minds, low or no SI, ignorance. It is also evidence we are not as civilized as we would like to think.

7. SPIRITUAL GROWTH DRIVE

This is Aristotle's "need to know," Einstein's "holy curiosity," Teilhard's hominization to Omega, and Maslow's need for self-actualization. In *Four quartets,* T.S. Eliot wrote: "We shall never cease from exploration and the end of all our exploring will be to arrive where we started and know the place for the first time." SI is more yearning than learning, coming from within, not doing what's expected, role behavior, or to impress others. Those with it are spiritual "grownups" seeking "the wisdom of the ages" in a spiritual journey. Hindus call them "old souls."

The fact you are reading this book suggests you have this S-trait. Other signs are a fascination about people, cultures, or other belief systems. It is a childlike loving curiosity with no need to know as a defense, a weapon, or power motive. It is being aware you don't know everything about yourself or about life and finding out means moving above and beyond yourself. It is more than developing a self-concept but rather reaching out and up to higher truth, Adam's hand outstretched to God's for the spark of truth.

8. SELFLESS SERVICE

People with high SI are selfless, not selfish. They give freely of themselves "without counting the cost" or getting anything in return. Words of thanks are not expected or needed. That is not why they give. They charge their spiritual batteries by giving. Life to them is more a mission than a career. Living is giving. Their pure motive is a deep love and caring. In his book *The Prophet*, Lebanese poet Kahlil Gibran wrote: "Work is love made visible." John Sullivan described it in his book *Servant first, leadership for the new millennium* (1991).

High SI people look at life as an opportunity to leave a job and the world better than they found it. They often say they have "a need to give something back." Work and chores are offerings, prayers in actions. Selfless service can be given alone or directly with and to people and to a higher power. It can be done in public or in secret, to friends and family, in help you don't really have to give. Often it goes unnoticed and unrewarded. Examples from history are Florence Nightingale, Albert Schweitzer, Mohandas Gandhi, and Mother Teresa.

9. MODESTY, HUMILITY

This S-trait is reflected in the self-effacing manner of Jesus, Gandhi, Schweitzer, Mother Teresa, and Lincoln. Maslow called it "grandiose humility that makes possible transcendence of self" (1968). Strangely, greatness shines through their humility. In the *New Testament* Jesus pointed to a small child saying: "Whoever humbles himself like this child is the greatest in the kingdom of God" (*Matthew* 18:4). Socrates' "prayer" reported by Plato in *Phaedo* is another example of this S-trait:

> Beloved Pan and all other gods who
> haunt this place, give me beauty in
> my inner soul, and may my outer and
> inner being be one. Help me realize
> the wise are wealthy, may I have such
> of that wealth as is reasonable. "

Having this trait is being an "old shoe" person, one who is "easy to get along with" like wearing a pair of old shoes. It is wearing your knowledge like a pair of old shoes, not imposing it on others like wearing stiff new shoes. Jesus, St, Francis of Assisi, Joan of Arc, Lincoln, Washington, Gandhi, and Mother Teresa were old shoes. What shoes are you wearing?

10. COMPASSION, CARING

Buddha referred to this as loving kindness. Carl Rogers called it unconditional positive regard." Those with it accept all men and women as brothers and sisters, all children as their children, members of the same family.

To them, everyone and everything has a purpose. They are as caring as the Good Samaritan, to anyone in need. Maslow's "transcenders" have this S-trait. A quick self-test is how much you accept others as spiritual beings with unlimited potential.

11. POSITIVE ATTITUDE

In adverse circumstances those with this trait choose to be positive. They see and relate to the good in others as Will Rogers' did when he said: "I never met a man I didn't like." This S-trait is reflected in songs such as "Look for the silver lining" and "Just direct your feet to the sunny side of the street." Edward Everett Hale described it in his poem *Ten times one is ten* (1870):

> To look up and not down.
> To look forward and not back,
> To look out and not in, and
> To lend a hand.

Those with high SI see negatives but choose to be positive anyway. Doing so is to them as much moral as it is rational. They transform the negative into the positive by good deeds, kind words, and seeing and doing what is positive even in the most negative situations. Former Secretary of State Colin Powell kept this saying on his desk: "Optimism is a force multiplier." An eight-ounce glass with four ounces of water is half full, not half empty.

The **miracle question** is a therapy technique that applies this thinking. Ask yourself: If I awoke tomorrow with no problems, how would I know it? What would be the first sign? Who would notice? What would I be like?" Your answers can bring new insight about needs and wishes. Focus on that last question and take time to describe yourself without those problems. How can you be like that *right now*? Shakespeare's advice: "Assume a virtue though you have it not and by practice make it so." There's nothing wrong with role playing a better you, enacting how you really want to be, the best you, until it becomes the real you.

A test of this S-trait is how often and how well you choose to be positive when things go wrong. You can use failures as lessons of what to avoid in the future. To develop this trait, try to find something positive in every situation. Having it doesn't mean ignoring negatives. You have to be aware of negatives to find positives. In the *Qu'ran* is written: "Be patient, for the promise of God is true; do not let those who are uncertain divert you" (*Rome, 60*). Can you put a percentile on how often you choose to think and feel positively in difficult situations?

12. ELEGANT SIMPLICITY

Simplicity is an ancient standard. LaoTse referred to it in the *Book of Tao* 2500 years ago and Rudyard Kipling asked: "Teach us delight in simple things." In *War and Peace* Leo Tolstoy wrote: "There is no greatness where there is not simplicity, goodness, and truth." Great art and literature, drama, and music have an elegant simplicity. The Golden Rule, Ten Commandments, and the parables of Buddha and Jesus, even the Declaration of Independence and Gettysburg Address, are elegant in their simplicity. Hippocrates summed up all one needs to know about ethics in three words: "Do no harm."

A beautiful flower is elegant in its simplicity. Elegant simplicity is beyond "simplicity" as fine embroidery is beyond plain linen. A divine spark is emitted in artistry, craftsmanship as well as in simple acts of kindness. The quotes throughout this book are elegant in their simplicity. To further develop this S-trait use simpler language in your work and everyday life. Strive for elegance. LaoTse in *the book of Tao* compared careful speech to a person stepping carefully across a frozen stream in winter. Tread lightly. Use just the right word at the right time in the right way. There is elegance, too, in silence. Buddha said if you have nothing to add, say nothing.

13. SPONTANEITY

Those with this S-trait know themselves to such an extent they freely express their thoughts and feelings. Their free expression can be mistaken for being unthinking or uncaring. Others not as spontaneous may feel uneasy being with them. Jacob Moreno, founder of psychodrama, felt spontaneity is a major part of mental health. High SI people tend to be free spirits even in restrictive settings. Maslow said "pure spontaneity is not long possible in a world of non-psychic laws, but then pure control is also not always possible and varies with the health of the psyche and the world." Carl Sandburg described it succinctly: "There is the authoritative instant and the moment of freedom and they are always killing each other."

The measure of this S-trait is its opposite, the degree of self-control or over-control. Being spontaneous does not mean reckless abandon. That is irresponsible and not a feature of high SI. It is being relaxed with yourself such that you are truly yourself wherever you are. Other words for it are being genuine, authentic, whole, or together. To what extent are you a free spirit? You need to be free to develop a higher consciousness.

14. HONEST CANDOR

Honest candor is direct communications and may seem impertinent or insulting. Those with it are "honest to a fault," open and sincere. They have no other motive than to "tell it like it is" without malice or intent to hurt anyone's feelings. In a 1778 letter, George Washington wrote of his hope to have "firmness and virtue enough to maintain what I consider the most enviable of all titles, the character of an honest man." In his 1734 *Essay on man,* Alexander Pope recognized it as a special, even holy trait: "An honest man's the noblest work of God." There is a down side. In *Othello*, Shakespeare commented "to be direct and honest is not safe." Norman Vincent Peale described the risk: "Twist the truth and make a hit. Tell the truth and get hit."

There is honest candor in relating to others openly and directly, to disagree without being disagreeable, and in facing differences rather than denying or avoiding them. Everyone is entitled to an opinion and in fact has a right to be wrong. Having this trait is being true to yourself as well as to others. Those with high SI tend to apologize when giving opinions because they care about people, even those with whom they disagree. Honest candor also involves striving to match your truth to higher truth. Otherwise, you're only reinforcing your opinions.

15. SPIRITUAL INTROJECTION

Introjection is the ability to "take in" what you are thinking and feeling and what is happening to you. It   is to open and maintain a meditative awareness bank of spiritual earnings within yourself. A self-test is how much time you spend reflecting on and absorbing the spiritual aspects of everyday life.

This trait is distinctive by its in-depth inward search for spiritual truth. Optimizing your SI is an intrapsychic process. It begins by looking within oneself for unmet spiritual needs. These needs are processed by meditative awareness and absorbed (introjected). Spiritual energy is generated in this process that also expands consciousness. This is transformational and transcending and the spiritual quality that distinguishes it from the self-actualization in Maslow's model. This S-trait is not the same as introversion. Introverts may find it easier but extroverts are also capable of using it.

16. SPIRITUAL HUMOR

Humor warms, uplifts, and transforms mood and outlook. It can warm, elevate and transform mood and outlook. Humor can help simplify what is complex, desensitize what is sensitive, and transcend bias and differences. It has transforming power to help laugh at foolishness, pride, and move to deeper reflective thought Maslow referred to a trait he called "playfulness." Those with high SI have a sense of humor with a distinctive spiritual quality.

Maslow saw a spiritual dimension in humor: "This special kind of playfulness has a comic or godlike, good-humored quality transcending hostility, simultaneously mature and childlike." Jesus used humor in irony when he said to men about to stone a prostitute: "Let him who is without sin cast the first stone." There are drawings of a laughing Jesus, unlike the usual depictions of him. Why not? Many Zen koans help us laugh at ourselves and often use sarcasm to trigger satori flashes of insight.

This S-trait is similar to the playfulness in childlike innocence. It is gracious, never hurtful, and has a spiritual quality. A smile is a sign of good humor. There is a spiritual quality in the face of a sleeping baby or even in the smile of a stranger passing by. Watch for them! Their effect is contagious. There can be "sacred smiles" to birds and animals, flowers and trees, sky and clouds, sunsets and sunrises. Clowns represent the joy of children, the Eternal Child within each of us. Do you "clown around," laugh at and with life, and give sacred smiles? Try to find and reflect on something funny every day. If you can't find anything, do something funny yourself.

EXERCISE 5. *It may help you to review the S-traits and watch for opportunities to experience them in your daily life.*

OVERLAP: DIVINE DIFFUSION?

S-traits overlap and complement each other. They are synergistic by exceeding the sum of individual features. That additive power is a feature of the divine spark from God or the higher power of the universe, a divine diffusion. Developing one trait helps develop others. Blended they optimize SI and enrich perception to separate the mundane from the meaningful. They energize the movement upward to higher consciousness. S-traits reflect the nature and dynamics of what is truly spiritual. In a 2000 journal article, Howard Gardner described three *connotations* of the word spiritual:

1. A physical state with "concomitants such as intelligence."

2. Reaching "certain phenomenological states" such as losing one's self in "an oceanic state" or a "special link to God" but without emotion "since feelings are external to the intellectual realm."

3. Elements that transcend sensory perception that are "existential because it seems yoked to the fact of our existence and individuals in the cosmos and our capacity to puzzle over the fact."

Gardner's "connotations" show a cognitive bias and a denial of the emotional richness of spirituality. In the same journal, Robert Emmons defended SI, listing four core components: capacity for transcendence; a heightened consciousness; the "sacred or divine" in everyday activities, events, and relationships; and using spiritual resources to solve problems. The 16 S-traits support Emmons' components as also SI-rich material in the arts and humanities worldwide, across time and culture,

There are many examples of high SI in religious and political leaders throughout history. LaoTse, Buddha, and Patanjali (yoga) are exemplars in Asia, and Moses and Jesus in the Middle East. St. Francis of Assisi, Martin Luther, John Calvin, and John Wesley reflected S-traits on both sides of the Reformation. High SI is reflected in the writings of Ralph Waldo Emerson, William Ellery Channing, and Paul Tillich. In modern times Mohandas Gandhi, Mother Teresa, Thomas Merton, Paul Tillich, and Martin Luther King Jr. had the divine spark. SI is evident in political leaders as well, such as Franklin, Jefferson, and Lincoln despite personal weaknesses.

SI SPARKS

11. God expects one thing from us, that we let God be God in us (Meister Eckhart).
12. You are God's temple and God's spirit dwells in you (Paul, I *Corinthians* 3:16).
13. God is in me and all things are shadows of Him (Ralph Waldo Emerson).

14. The evidence for God lies primarily in inner personal experience (William James).
15. The leaf of a tree, the meanest insect on which we trample, are in themselves arguments more con-clusive than any which can be adduced that some vast intellect animates infinity (Percy Bysshe Shelley).
16. In the midst of winter I learned there was in me an invincible summer (Albert Camus, *Actuelles*, 1960)
17. The most important missing part in our life experience is a center. Without a center everything goes on in the periphery and there is no place from which to work, from which to cope with the world ("Fritz" Perls, *Gestalt therapy verbatim*, 1969).
18. We are always something more than we know of ourselves but in a process of life endowed with possibilities (Karl Jaspers, *Man in the modern era*, 1937).
19. Faith does not contradict reason. It transcends it (Mohandas Gandhi).
20. Spiritual rebirth is the key to the aspirations of all the higher religions (Thomas Merton, in *Love and living*, 1985).

3

SI IN THE WEST

We are born too late for
the old and too early for
the new faith.
-- Ralph Waldo Emerson

Western religion is mainly Judeo-Christian, with
many variations. Like Hindus and Buddhists in the East,
Jews and Christians have remained separate. This is ironic
since Jesus was a Jew and Buddha was Hindu. SI connects
all of them and all the offshoots. That includes major
schisms and sectarian differences. Applying the 16 S-traits
to developing religions helps explain the dynamics of
change. All major religions have had schisms: Orthodox,
Conservative, and Reform Judaism; Roman Catholic and
Protestant Christianity; Mahayana, Hinayana, and Zen
Buddhism; and Shi'ia and Sunni Islam.

Conflict is likely when a sect cannot accept change. As
the number of people seeking change grows, so also does
the risk of schism. The result can be extensive, such as
Protestant Reformation or minor such as founding a new
religious order or specialty subgroup. Examples of
subgroups are Hassidic Jews, Sufi Muslims, and the many
religious orders of Roman Catholic priests, nuns, and
monks. Most religions follow a fixed system of rules and
beliefs. Once the system is set it is difficult to make
changes. When a sect claims to be the only source of truth
it isolates itself. The result in the West has been

a splitting into hundreds of Christian sects from snake handling to the Catholic mass and destructive cults that killed hundreds.

Even in the most orthodox religions change is evident over time. To provide a worldwide standard the Catholic mass was in Latin. It is now "in the vernacular," in the language of each country. Doctrinal differences occurred as a reaction to "heretics." Church leaders who won the debate were usually sainted, such as when Augustine overcame the metaphysical slant of Origen. From the second to the sixth centuries "patristic theology" held sway. Later, theology adapted or reacted to scholasticism, medieval mysticism, and the Counter-reformation.

It may seem surprising a theologian would be critical of Western religion. Paul Tillich, in a 1958 *Saturday Evening Post* article *The lost dimension in religion*, said: "Western religion has become a non-religion and the first step was made by religion itself." He added: "It had already lost the battle when it defended great symbols not as symbols but as literal stories."

SI in the West dimmed after a good beginning in the golden age of Greece in the 6th century BCE and the insight of Socrates, Plato, and Aristotle. The Crusades from 1095 to 1204 CE were wars over religion, with little or no SI to light the way to peace. Muslims and Christians acted on their differences and refused to use what they shared. It is interesting to note Islam accepts Moses and Jesus but Christianity excludes Judaism and Islam. More interesting is the rise of Muslim terrorism, a radical departure from the *Qu'ran*, in a religion that accepts Judaism and Christianity.

Founders of world religions didn't have the time or means to fully define themselves or their truth. Well meaning followers were one or more steps removed from the divine spark the founder received. Questions grew and attempts at answers raised even more questions. Differences grew along with other problems. There was no clear separation of church and state in the Christian world. That increased the risk of self-interest and power struggles.

In *Anatomy of melancholy* (1621) Robert Burton wrote: "Where God has a temple the devil has a chapel." The Crusades began in 1095 CE and ended in the late 13th century. They were among the longest and bloodiest religious wars in history. Armies battled to protect their faith and overcome those of another faith.

The Crusades were a failure for both sides except for taking and retaking Jerusalem and Constantinople. On the positive side, the Crusades opened trade between west and east that enriched both sides. The exchange of ideas helped pave the way to the Renaissance. On the negative side, thousands died and many more suffered. Even today the word Crusade is used by Muslim extremists to fan the flames of hatred against the United States, "the great Satan."

The Inquisition in the Middle Ages is an example of how a well-meaning majority can do evil. Catholicism became the state religion in the Roman Empire in the 4th century. Heretics were punished by excommunication. As time passed, opinion hardened about how to deal with the problem. In 1231 CE Pope Gregory IX established what became known as The Inquisition in Germany and France. Inquisitors were usually Dominicans or Franciscans because of their training in theology. They would arrive in a community and announce their presence. People guilty of heresy could turn themselves in. In most cases that meant a lesser penalty. Trials were by a jury of clergy and laity. Those found guilty received sentences from penance and a fine to life imprisonment and confiscation of property.

In 1252 CE Pope Innocent IV approved torture if inquisitors felt the accused withheld information. In 1478 CE the Spanish Inquisition was established at the request of King Ferdinand V and Queen Isabella I. Tomas Torquemada was the first Grand Inquisitor. He was more rigorous and punitive than previous authorities. Many were tortured or killed during his term. By the 16th century the Inquisition softened and turned its attention to correcting group misbelief, mostly in Italy. In 1559 CE the first *Index of Forbidden Books* was issued. It was the basis for charging Galileo with heresy for stating the earth revolved around the sun. Inquisitions were not limited to Roman Catholicism. The Geneva Consistory executed alleged heretics.

From 1409 to 1417 there were three popes. From 1447 to 1517 half the popes sired children. The plague in 1347 CE killed 40% of the people. The hundred years' war 1353 to 1453 CE between England and France was followed by the thirty year Wars of the Roses. The Muslim army took Constantinople and moved into the Balkans. If the plague was the wrath of God, what were the wars? Durer portrayed the dark mood of the time in his painting *Four horsemen of the apocalypse.*

Still, there was some light. Marsilius of Padua (c. 1275-1342) suggested a bottom-up system from the people, today's Protestant congregation governed model. The

Church moved toward councils of cardinals, but the majority was Italian. St. Francis of Assisi (1182-1226 CE) was a living model of piety and poverty. The Franciscans became a powerful force for reform. Dutch and German Augustinians stressed the need for more faith and less worldly concern. Martin Luther was an Augustinian. In England, John Wycliffe (c. 1320-1384 CE) translated the Bible from Latin to English, making it available to the people.

The reform movement spread throughout Europe. Jan Hus (1373-1415 CE), a priest, furthered Wycliffe's cause in Bohemia. He was excommunicated, declared a heretic, and executed by the state in 1415. Luther said in 1520: "Without knowing it I taught and held the teaching of Hus. We were all Hussites without knowing it." There was a spiritual hunger at these times. Mystic thought grew, as it has in all major world religions. It is as if SI continues its divine spark despite any limits put on it. The wish to enlighten and empower people led to more humanism. Erasmus (c. 1469-1536 CE), son of a priest, was a prime mover in this movement that humanized Jesus and urged people to use him as a role model.

Alchemy, magic, sorcery, and astrology were practiced in early Christianity but in the 13th century were seen as having evil potential. Pope Alexander IV expanded the Inquisition to include witchcraft. Anyone outside mainstream society was suspect, such as unmarried, unchurched, reclusive women. Any eccentric could be accused of casting spells when there was a drought, plague, sick cow, or sexually impotent husband. Those found to be witches were referred to civil courts for prosecution. From 470 to 1700 thousands were executed, usually burned at the stake. Many confessed after being tortured.

In 1486 CE two Dominican inquisitors wrote the *The witch's hammer (Malleus Maleficarum).* It was a manual for detecting satanic behavior in witches. It defined witchcraft as "high treason against God's majesty." It justified torture "to make them confess." Among the signs of witchcraft: an area of the body insensitive to pain, inability to cry, extra nipples, and floating in water. Sinking proved innocence. The book was second only to the *Bible* in readership in both Catholic and Protestant countries.

Puritans came to the new world to escape religious intolerance but fell victim to witch hysteria in 1692 CE. It began when the 9-year-old daughter of minister Samuel Parris "sickened." She forgot errands and chores, had a blank stare, difficulty concentrating, and "swooned, babbled, and screamed." It spread to her 11-year-old cousin. She would convulse or drop on all fours and bark like a dog. A 12-year-old showed similar behaviors. Starkey (1949) described the girls as "finding relief for their tensions in an emotional orgy."

Reverend Parris took the girls to a physician who concluded "the evil hand is on them." Cotton Mather, popular Puritan clergyman, fed the hysteria with the Biblical admonitions "thou shalt not suffer a witch to live" and "there shall not be among you anyone who useth divination or is a witch" (*Deuteronomy* 18:10). The trials were held by two lay magistrates. The jury stripped suspects naked and looked for "devil marks." They stuck pins in any body part that looked suspicious. *Spectral evidence* allowed at trial were fantasies, dreams, and even thoughts of the devout about suspects. By the time the

Salem witch hunt ended 20 men and women died. Their legal wills were voided and their property confiscated.

Sarah Good was charged with killing cows by mumbling curses and sickening children by calling them names. She gave birth in prison. The baby died. Sarah Osburne, sickly and probably senile, died in prison. Martha Cory, an outspoken woman, was convicted. Giles, her husband, was "pressed to death" with rocks on his chest after he refused to testify against her. Dorcas Good was hanged. Her 5-year-old daughter was orphaned. Captain John Alden of Longfellow's poem was charged but acquitted. Convicted witches and male wizards were hanged every week. It was a public spectacle always well attended.

The risk of extremes increases when a religion becomes the majority. In *Faith and violence* (1968) Thomas Merton explained: "If we love our own ideology and our own opinion instead of loving our brother we will seek only to glorify our own ideas and our institutions and by that fact make real communication impossible" (p. 163).

The Protestant Reformation and Catholic Counter Reformation showed neither side could adapt or adjust to reality. One defended the old because it stood the test of time. The other fought for the new because it satisfied current needs. There was truth on both sides. Neither side won. Today's religion-based violence suggests all sides are still losing. This is true in the East as well, for Hindu and Muslim in the Kashmir and Sunni and Shia Muslim in Iraq. There seems to be a worldwide SI blackout.

Unlike religion, SI is open and freely incorporates knowledge regardless of its source to move toward a higher consciousness and a mystic unity that transcends differences. SI is the means to that end and not a religion. It enriches both religion and science and also enriches the search for personal and spiritual meaning.

SI EAST AND WEST

There is a difference in how West and East develop SI. The East seeks enlightenment, insight, and wisdom by an internal focus on *mental processes*. The West is more social, with group norms of morality and conduct, an external focus on *behavior*. Time is more important in the West but only relative in the East. Ask a Zen master when your studies will be finished and you're apt to be told: "When the apple is ripe it will drop from the tree of its own weight." The East is unhurried. It is timeless. The West is impatient, nervously seeking "fast food" short cuts to truth.

On the plus side, the West has led the world in science and technology. On the minus side its weaponry has led to the conquest of other lands. It has destroyed and sought to replace other religions, presuming it alone owned truth. It did not preserve or learn from other belief systems. The West is younger. Like brash youth, it sees intelligence more as *school smarts*.

The East is much older and at a higher level of SI, *spiritual smarts*. It has had much more time to develop SI. It is as if the West boasts: "I'm an A student" and the East whispers: "I'm a student." Or, as if the West has put more food for the body on the table and the East puts more food for the spirit in the mind. The West has been more into its head, thinking more than feeling, the East more into its heart, feeling as well as thinking. The West is far more *compulsive* and this has resulted in great scientific and technological progress. The East has been more *obsessive*, resulting in deeper spiritual awareness. Each has strengths and weaknesses:

EAST	WEST
slower pace	faster pace
quietly reflective	vocal, reactive
internalized	externalized
indirect	direct
inductive	deductive
conserving	consuming

Which is better? The West would likely answer: "Let's take a test!" The East might reply: "Why test or choose?" An SI answer, based on the wide scope of history might be: "Neither and both." Science can refine religion and SI by testing and research. Religion can enrich science by helping it find a moral compass, a unifying philosophy that ennobles and does not demean what is human. Buddha showed that such a blending is possible in his four noble truths and eightfold path, described in the next chapter.

EXERCISE 6. *How much "Eastern" perspective do you have or could you have in your daily life? If you see an advantage in it, reflect on ways in your daily routine you can apply the Eastern view more, every day.*

MYSTICISM

Mysticism seeks a direct personal link to God. It has many names: mystic unity, the mystic bond, cosmic consciousness. It may surprise you that Frank Sinatra gave a good definition of mysticism in a 1963 interview. He was asked about his religious belief and he replied: "Religion is a deeply rooted personal thing in which man and God go it alone together without a witch doctor in the middle." Henri Bergson wrote in his 1932 book *Dynamic religion*: "Religion is crystallization cooled by science, what mysticism pours while hot into the soul."

There is some mystic thought in all world religions. Mohandas Gandhi wrote in *Young India* (1921): "God reveals Himself daily to us but we shut our ears to the still small voice." In ancient Greece, Heraclitus of Ephesus observed: "The god who speaks through the oracle at Delphi neither reveals nor conceals but imparts meaning in hints." The mystic saint, John of the Cross, wrote in his first *Spiritual Canticle*: "God is unapproachable, hidden, and however much you seem to find and understand Him you must ever hold Him as hidden and serve Him in hidden ways as one who is hidden."

There is risk of error in searching for hidden meaning. Religions have shown more presumption and orthodoxy than proven fact. It has caused conflict and war. Though well-intentioned, missionaries have replaced belief systems, presuming theirs is the only religious truth. Not all believers were so rigid. John Wesley, founder of Methodism, wrote in his *Journal*: "My own belief is not the rule for another." And Buddha taught followers to greeting others with: "This is what we believe. Accept it or decline. Either way, peace be with you."

SI IN JUDAISM
THE KABBALAH

The *Kabbalah*, also known as *Cabala* or *Qabalah*, has been called "the yoga of the West" and the key to the mysteries of the universe. Its precise origin is not known. Legend traces it to Abraham. Scholars find it to be a blend of Alexandrian and Palestinian Judaism with some ideas from Gnostic Christian, Pythagorean Greek, Egyptian, and yoga. It emerged between the 2nd and 6th centuries CE. It was a major influence to mystic thought in the Middle Ages and Reformation.

The *Kabbalah* is believed to connect with the astral or spirit body of *Ein-sof* (infinite God). It dies this by way of the "sacred tree" of *ten emanations* (aspects, levels, stages) called the *Sefirot*. The emanations are aspects of the infinite. There are two versions of the *Kabbalah*. One is the *Book of Formation* (*Sefer Yetzirah*). The other is the *Book of Splendor* (*Sefer ha-Zohar*) thought to be written by Moses de Leon in 1275 CE. *Gematria* is a branch of Kabbalistic study that converts Hebrew words into numerals and uses them to form mystic concepts.

Kether (crown), the one infinite God or absolute is at the top of the "tree" of the ten emanations. It is said to be beyond rational understanding or even ecstatic contemplation. It is approached with "mystical agnosticism" (Scholem, 1974). Beneath *Kether* are two emanations that form a triangle with *Kether*. On the left is *Binah*, mother force of understanding and knowing without facts. On the right is *Hokhmah*, father force of wisdom and knowing what seems a cause of events can conceal ultimate reality. Beneath them are two others: *Geburah* on the left, feminine "just love," symbolized by Mars, and *Chesed* on the right, masculine "protective love," symbolized by Jupiter.

Tiferet is centered beneath *Geburah* and *Chesed*. It is glory in "radiant beauty and elegance" and inner serenity of "emotional sublimation." Its symbol is the sun. Two emanations are beneath *Tiferet*: *Hod* on the left, of honor and majesty, and *Nisah* or *Nezah* on the right, of endurance and victory. Centered beneath them is the *Yesod* of firm foundations. Its symbol is the moon. Centered beneath it is *Malchut* or *Malkut,* of earth and physical realities. Its symbol is the rainbow and nature. The ten emanations are linked by 22 lines, each of which is a way to study the *Kabbalah.*

Kabbalah study begins with *Malkut* at the base of the sacred tree and moves upward. *Yesod* is achieved by good conduct, meditation, and prayer on seeing "form and not realities." *Hod* is realized by "the joy giving up mundane selfish thoughts." *Nezah* is attained "rising above emotion and abandoning the mind to its own devices." *Tiferet* is realized by developing the inner serenity of "emotional sublimation." *Geburah* is reached by moving upward without reason and logic. To know *Ein-sof* or *Kether* one must achieve nothing-everything and transcend the great void.

DEAD SEA SCROLLS

The Essenes lived in desert communes in the Qumran area until dispersed by the Roman legions of Vespasian in 67 CE. They called themselves "sons of light." We learned of them in 1947 when a Bedouin shepherd boy found them in a remote cave. They are rolls and fragments of copper, parchment, or dried skins of goat, ibex, or cow. Many were darkened by age or stained by bat guano and animal urine. They were the rules of the Essenes, hymns, prayers, esoteric prophecies, and an almost complete Hebrew Bible. Before 1947 little was known of them except for brief references by the Roman Pliny the Elder and Jewish writers Josephus and Philo of Alexandria. They described Essenes as an isolated Jewish commune 200 BCE to 200 CE.

The scrolls describe a strict group whose members lived a reflective life. There were degrees of membership conferred by member vote. Purity and piety were valued as signs of higher consciousness. They wore white and practiced ritual baths and prayers. Casual conversation was forbidden. Members shared property and worked at farming or handicrafts. The blind, deaf, and lame were excluded because they believed they might frighten away angels and one must be able to see and hear to study well. Though Jewish, their baptism ritual and belief in imminent end of the world are consistent with the *New Testament*.

The scrolls were written at a time of ferment and conflict with competing messianic movements. The *Torah* was taught by mentors called "teachers of righteousness." Teachings referred to people by role and not by name: "man of lies, wicked priest, persecuted teacher, children of light." They expected a new prophet after a battle between "the sons of light" and "the sons of darkness." Sadly, it was the Roman legion and not the sons of darkness who came and in force. They believed they would prevail by divine power rather than weapons. It's likely they hid the scrolls faced with armed force and were killed or driven away leaving no one to return the scrolls.

The need to date, decipher, and preserve the scrolls formed an uneasy alliance between science and religion. Religion feared the scrolls might undermine Jewish and Christian belief systems. Science saw a new source of information about Jesus and his time. Despite the uneasy truce Jewish, Christian, and Muslim scholars collaborated with scientists. Carbon 14 dating confirmed their age at between 250 BCE to 150 CE, most between 100 BCE and 70 CE. Multispectral imaging in infrared light deciphered what was unreadable before. Neutron analysis of the clay pot containers found them to be locally made but with special care for a special purpose. The interaction of science and religion proved there can be close collaboration of benefit to both.

SI IN EARLY CHRISTIANITY
GNOSTICS

An ancient sealed jar was found in 1945 in the sands of the upper valley of the Nile River. In it were 52 ancient papyri now known as the *Nag Hammadi*. They were written by Gnostics, pre- and early Christians from 200 BCE to 200 CE. *Gnosis* is from the Greek for special or secret knowledge. Gnostics believed higher truth is hidden in language and literature. Like Kabbalists, their God or higher power was beyond words or simple understanding. They believed they could realize it by enriching their inner life which was part of God. To them, others were lost in the details and trivia of everyday life. Their goal was to free the spirit to find higher truth above and beyond everyday life yet still connected to it.

The *Nag Hammadi* papyri shed light on the earliest Christian teachings. Among them are the *Books* of *James* and *Thomas*, presumably Jesus' brothers. They contain sayings of Jesus not in the *New Testament*. Bible scholars now suspect Matthew and Luke wrote their gospels 15 to 20 years after Mark. Content analysis suggests they referred to Mark and other sources. Gnostics believed Jesus taught secret wisdom that was hidden in the surface content of what was said and done. Finding it achieved spiritual enlightenment. Here's a sample from *The Secret Teachings of Jesus* (Meyers, 1986):

1. Jesus said: "Show me the stone that was rejected by the builders. That is the cornerstone" (*Thomas, 66*).
2. If you do not know yourself you cannot learn well. Know yourself and you can know the universe (*Thomas, 112*).
3. The One is power over all, God and Father of all, invisible and eternal, pure light no eye can see. It is Spirit, not a god or like a god but greater than that, perfect, the light that is in everything eternally. It is limitless, nothing before it, after, above, or below it; immeasurable since it cannot be contained; invisible since it cannot be seen; nameless and unutterable since it is beyond words; and eternal, without beginning or end. It is the great light, bright, pure, holy, eternal, greater than great in perfection and holiness. It is beyond real and unreal, large or small, beyond understanding (*John 2:1-12*).
4. Why do you only wash the outside of the cup? Don't you understand who made the outside also made the inside? (*Thomas, 87*).
5. The Perfect One shows itself in the light surrounding it (*John 3:1*)
6. There is light in an enlightened person that shines on the whole world (*Thomas, 24*).
7. If asked where you come from answer: "We come from the light, where light created and sustained itself in its own image." If asked if you are the light say: "We are its children chosen of the living Father." If asked for proof answer: "It is in action and inaction" (*Thomas, 50*).
8. Trust in me and understand the great light (*James, 5-6*).

9. Let who hears awaken from a deep sleep (*John, 16:11*).
10. When you make two of one, the inner the outer and the outer the inner, male and female as one, eyes for eyes, hands for hands, feet for feet, and image for image, you will enter the Kingdom" (*Thomas, 22*).

CHRISTIAN MYSTICS

There is mystic content in the *New Testament* gospels, Paul's epistles, and the *Book of Revelations* thought to be written by John the Evangelist, "the beloved apostle." John was the last surviving apostle and had more time to reflect on what Jesus said and did. His gospel differs from others by its mystic quality and figurative language. John wrote of Jesus' divine qualities and how to share in it for spiritual growth. Scholars suspect he may not have written *Revelations* since it differs in style from his gospel and is future-oriented, not framed in the present. This is not unusual and doesn't lower the value or weaken the meaning of what is written. Content analysis of the Bible and other world scriptures show similar differences and suggest multiple writers.

A sample of John's mystic thought: "The light shines in the darkness but the darkness has not understood it" (1:5). No one can see the kingdom of God unless he is born again (3:3). I am the bread of life (6:35). You will know the truth and the truth will set you free (8:32).

There were other mystic saints; Augustine, Aquinas, Francis of Assisi, John of the Cross, Catherine of Siena, Teresa Avila, Meister Eckhart, and Hildegard von Bingen. Christian mystic thought dates back to Dionysius Areopagiticus, a 1st century Athenian converted by Paul. He described a "divine void" similar to the Kabbalah's *kether* or *Ein-sof* and Buddhist *shunyata*. His Greek teachings were translated into Latin and spread through European monasteries.

Catherine of Siena said she "merged with an ocean of rest." Meister Eckhart described "the peaceful silence that enwraps all things." Spanish mystic John of the Cross said he descended by selfless humility into total emptiness, darkness, and reflective silence and it was only then he experienced divine love. Teresa of Avila called her mystic experience *transverberation.* She envisioned her chest pain as an angel's fiery sword to her heart bringing the ecstasy of God's love. Episcopal priest Alan Watts and Roman Catholic monk Thomas Merton wrote of mystical aspects of religious practice.

THE LABYRINTH

The word labyrinth is from the Greek *labyrinthos.* A labyrinth is an intricate, confusing design of passageways and blind alleys with only one way to the center. It can be built in gardens with tall closely spaced shrubs, by fences or walls, or in caves. There is a level labyrinth set in the floor of the Chartres cathedral in France. It is used as a prayer aid. Walking through it is a symbolic spiritual pilgrimage. Some believe labyrinths generate a positive force. Labyrinths have also been used to meditate on a personal problem, troubling emotion, the meaning of life, and to further develop meditative awareness.

There is an ancient labyrinth in caves on the island of Crete. According to legend, they were built by Daedalus for King Minos, son of Zeus and Europa. He built them to imprison the minotaur. It was half man half bull and killed and ate people. The hero Theseus, king of Athens, entered the cave and killed it. He found his way in and out by following a thread given him by Ariadne, daughter of

King Minos. He unwound the thread as he moved through the cave.

SI IN ANCIENT GREECE
ASKLEPIOS

The **cult of Asklepios** flourished in Greece 2500 years ago. It spread to Rome as the cult of Aesculapius and was a major competitor to early Christianity. According to Greek legend, *Asklepios* was "the most humane of the gods." He was the son of *Apollo* and *Coronis*, a sign of great power and importance. *Chiron*, centaur at Mount Pelion, was his mentor. It is likely *Asklepios* was a living person. *Homer* reported he was a person renowned for great kindness and compassion who helped the sick.

Hippocrates was an Asklepian priest-physician on the island of Kos in 300 BCE. Today the *Hippocratic Oath* is still sworn by graduating physicians just as it was by medical students in ancient Greece. *Hippocrates* was a man of great ability and insight. More than 2000 years ago he knew diseases have natural and not supernatural causes. In Europe during the Middle Ages it was believed mental illness was demonic possession. *Hippocrates* classified disease as acute or chronic illness and mild, moderate, or severe. He also taught a simple code of ethics: "Do no harm," still a useful standard.

Greek and Roman Asklepian temples (*asklepiads*) were visited by those seeking cures for medical conditions or peace of mind for mental distress. Leaders in government, medicine, philosophy, and literature participated in the rituals. *Marcus Aurelius* prayed there for his mentor *Sophocles*. *Socrates'* last words to *Plato* showed that he valued them: "I owe a cock to *Asklepios*. Do not neglect to pay it." *Alexander the Great* made a pilgrimage to

Epidauros, the major Asklepian center where *Asklepios* was believed to have been born.

Asklepian practices are consistent with ways to optimize SI. Temples were located outside cities, usually on high ground, near a natural spring and grove of trees. Over the entrance was inscribed: "Only the pure enter here." To be pure was "to have none but pure thoughts." That also meant being physically clean. One would bathe in the nearby spring to prepare physically and mentally for treatment. Temple grounds were a restful setting. Walking from the dormitory to the temple helped set a reflective mood.

There were columns across the front and sides of the temple. Floors were of alternating light and dark marble tiles. Doors were inlaid with ivory and studded with gold nails. Inside the temple was a statue of Asklepios as an older bearded man, standing, and with "far seeing eyes." In his right hand was the omphalos, sphere of unity with the absolute. In his left hand he held the caduceus, a long staff with two entwined snakes, tongues touching the god's fingertip. The snake was the symbol of immortality and rebirth because they shed their skin for a new life.

Priest-physicians welcomed people to the temple and took a history of their problems and needs. Prayers, hymns, or poems were given along with offerings of figs, honey cakes, or baked meats. Massage and exercise might be prescribed. At night, people slept in the temple on pallets. Another statue of *Asklepios* was there, seated and calming a lion with a fixed stare. Asklepiads were called "temples of sleep." It was hoped the god would appear in "dream sleep" and tell or signify treatment. Some scholars suspect a priest dressed as *Asklepios* moved among the people, with a dog and now extinct gold-colored snake. It has been suggested the dog may have licked wounds and the snake was a symbol of mystic wisdom.

Dream healing was valued more than a priest's advice, though the priest would help interpret the god's message. Treatment included herbal ointments and compresses but the most important was dream healing. The priest's role much like what Freud described as "a midwife assisting at the birth of the new individual." The priest interpreted dreams or whispered a cure as the patient slept. The cults of Asklepios, Isis, and Mithras were major competitors to Christianity until the 3rd century CE.

SI IN ANCIENT PERSIA
THE MAGI

The *magi* were *Zoroastrian* priests in Pars, the ancient name for Persia, now Iraq. *Zoroaster* or *Zarathustra* was the founder of this ancient Persian religion. It flourished about the time of Cyrus in 550 BCE and declined after the invasion by Alexander the Great and the Muslims in the 7th century. Zoroastrians believed in one God who created two lesser gods: *Ormuzd,* who remained loyal and a force for good, and *Ahriman* who rebelled and became the force for evil.

Ormuzd created humans and things needed for a happy life. *Ahriman* created predatory birds and animals and poisonous snakes and plants. Thus good and evil coexist in constant conflict. Good was believed to be strongest. The forces for good were led by *Ahura Mazda,* god of wisdom and light. Evil forces were led by *Angra Mainyu,* god of the negative and darkness. The *magi* studied astronomy and paranormal phenomena, the basis of the legend of the "three wise men from afar" who brought gifts to the newborn Jesus. Parsees in northern India are descendants of those who fled from Alexander the Great and later Muslim invasions.

MITHRAS

The *cult of Mithras* began in Persia more than 5000 years ago. It spread to Greece, Babylonia, and the Roman Empire. *Mithras* was the half-god half-man mediator between humanity and *Ormuzd*, the god of good. Until the 3rd century it competed with early Christianity. The place of worship was most often a cave. *Mithras* was pictured kneeling on a bull with a dagger in his hand. The bull was the symbol of nature, instinct, and power. He was the symbol of the need to take action, control passion, and rise above instinct.

The *cult of Mithras* was a popular secret society in the Roman Legion. Candidates went through three degrees of rituals and lessons that were given verbally and never read or in writing. Among objects used in the ritual were a gold crown (symbol of the sun, God, or paranormal power), the figure of a bull (symbolizing animal instinct and power), and a club or sword (action and control). The bullfights in Spain and Mexico are modern day examples of Mithraic ritual and their continuing popularity reflects their deep roots. Due to their secrecy, little is known of the teachings and rituals of ancient cults. There were many in addition to the Mithraic, such as *Dionysian, Eleusinian, Orphean, Isis,* and *Pythagorean*. Their popularity suggests they met a special need. From the meager records and objects found we know the rituals were likely dramatic role plays of trauma or loss, the initiate or symbolic figure was victimized. There were tasks or a journey to challenge the candidate had to overcome.

SI IN ANCIENT EGYPT
ISIS AND OSIRIS

The *Osiris legend* was a major part of the funeral inscriptions in ancient Egypt. The deceased, male or female, was referred to as *Osiris*. It was hoped the dead would repeat that god's journey from life through death to eternal life. There were many other gods and legends. *Ra* was the sun-god and chief of the gods. *Nuut*, goddess of the sky, was his wife. *Seb*, earth-god, had an affair with *Nuut* who became pregnant. Enraged, *Ra* put a curse on *Nuut* she could never give birth any day of any year. The god *Hermes* won the 70th part of a year in a card game with the god *Selene*. A year was then 360 days, so *Hermes* won five days not covered by *Ra's* curse. He gave them to *Nuut* which changed the year to 365 days. *Nuut* gave birth to a male god she named *Osiris*.

According to legend, *Osiris* ruled Egypt well. He shared his wisdom in travels to many lands. His wife *Isis* and her sister *Nephthys* ruled when he was away. Once when he returned there was a great feast. *Seth*, his brother, god of the darkness, storms, and desert, tricked him into lying down in a large chest. *Seth* then slammed it shut and threw it into the Nile River. It floated to Byblos where it stuck in a tamarisk tree that grew around it. The king of Byblos unknowingly cut the tree down for a pillar in his palace. *Isis*, goddess of magic, retrieved the chest and brought Osiris back to life.

Seth opened the chest, cut *Osiris* into 14 parts, and scattered them throughout Egypt. Isis searched for and found them and used her magic and the power of her love to bring *Osiris* back to life. By dying then coming back to life he became the god of the dead and the underworld.

Isis and *Osiris* had a son, *Horus*, the *avenger of Osiris*, helmsman of the sunboat of the dead, and god of the horizon. His symbol, the all-seeing eye, is often painted on the bows of riverboats, and the falcon, often depicted in temples. The mythology of ancient Egypt's "children of the Nile" was a cheerful optimism of happy endings and happy new beginnings.

In ancient Egypt mummification (embalming) was developed so well it is difficult to duplicate it even today science and technology. They took special care to preserve bodies because they believed death begins a journey from western sunset through the underworld to the eastern sunrise of eternal life. The *Egyptian Book of the Dead* was the guidebook preparing the living for death and read to the newly dead to guide them with *Osiris'* help through the death journey.

It evolved from pyramid wall inscriptions from 2600 BCE or before, later set down on rolls of papyrus, parchment made from reeds, 14 to 18 inches wide and 20 to 90 feet long. Originally, it was entombed only with pharaohs or high officials but later shorter versions were entombed with those of lower caste. For centuries scribes copied and recopied them with a loss in quality.

What ancient Egypt left behind, the pyramids, tombs, temples, and art, impressed visitors, from as Herodotus, the 5th century BCE "father of history," Plutarch in the 1st century CE, through Napoleon's 1812 CE invasion, to today's tourists. Herodotus referred to an old Egyptian scribe who told him: "Compared to us, you Greeks are but children." It is said Pythagoras (c. 530 BCE) spent almost 20 years studying Egyptian philosophy and mathematics.

Sadly, his works were lost when the Library of Alexandria burned down. Some estimate a million volumes were lost.

EXERCISE 7. *Review the Western religions and rate yourself in three columns: those you like, those you dislike, and those you neither like nor dislike. What does it tell you about your preferences in a religion? Your openness? Can you accept spirituality in those who differ from you in religion, language, and culture?*

SI SPARKS

21. Fix reason firmly in her seat and call to her tribunal every fact, every opinion. Question with boldness even the existence of a God because if there be one He must more approve the homage of reason than blindfolded fear (Thomas Jefferson, a 1787 letter to nephew Peter Carr).

22. Make your own Bible. Select and collect all the words and sentences that have been to you like the blast of trumpet out of Shakespeare, Seneca, Moses, John, and Paul (Ralph Waldo Emerson, *Journal*, 1836).

23. Scripture and religions have grown out of you and may grow out of you still. It is not they who give the life, it is you who give the life (Walt Whitman, *Leaves of grass*, 1855).

24. We have just enough religion to make us hate but not enough to make us love one another (Jonathan Swift, 1711, *Thoughts on various subjects*).

25. The end of all religion is not states of feeling but transformation of the personality (Anton Boisen, *Exploration of the inner world*, 1936).

26. I say the whole earth and all the stars in the sky are for religion's sake (Walt Whitman).

27. First, there is only one God who is perfect. Second, there is a future state of rewards and punishments. Third, to love God with all your heart and your neighbor as yourself. That is the sum of religion (Thomas Jefferson).
28. There is no god higher than truth (Mohandas Gandhi).
29. One universe of all that is, one God in it all, one principle of being, one law, reason, shared by all, and one truth (Marcus Aurelius, 121-189 BCE, *Meditations VII*).
30. Religions are all so many paths leading to the same goal. The universal religion is realizing God in the soul (Swami Vivekananda).

4

SI IN THE EAST

In many lands and many tongues
Buddha gave Asia light, conquering
the world with a spirit of strong
grace. (Edwin Arnold, *Light of Asia*)

Compared to the West, Asian Eastern religions and philosophies are more abstract and mystical. They focus more on individual development and a higher spiritual consciousness. In his book *Science and the modern world* (1925) Alfred North Whitehead wrote: "Christianity always has been religion seeking metaphysics. Buddhism is metaphysics that generated a religion" and "Buddhism is the most classical example in history of applied metaphysics." Of the founders of the major religions, Buddha was more consistent with psychology, even to today's theories and therapies.

Many personality theorists have been influenced by Eastern thought. Among them: Alexander, Binswanger, Boss, Bucke, Fromm, Goleman, Jung, Maslow, Murphy, Ornstein, Perls, and Tart. Asian thought has a longer history than the West. They had a thousand years more to test ideas and ways to develop SI. Unlike the West, there is more sharing and blending. There is an old Chinese saying: "One should wear a Confucian hat, a Taoist robe, and Buddhist sandals." In other words, be Confucian in the outside world, Buddhist on the 8-fold path of personal growth, and Taoist within yourself and the universe. Because they share much similar meanings,

Hinduism, Buddhism, Zen, and Taoism are presented together here.

HINDUISM

Hinduism is the major religion of India and one of the world's oldest. *Brahman* is its term for the supreme power or creator-god and *Atman* is the Brahmanic manifestation in each person. Within *Brahman* is the trinity (*trimurti*): *Brahman; Vishnu,* cosmic mind and preserver; and *Shiva,* cosmic lord and destroyer.

Shiva has four arms and is often shown dancing on the dwarf of ignorance. In *Shiva's* left hand is the flame of enlightenment and the other points to the uplifted left foot of release and progress. One right arm beats the drum of time, the other is palm up, accepting and reassuring. *Shiva* has a dual identity: *Kali* or *Durga*, goddess of death and destruction, and *Parvati* or *Uma*, goddess of birth, life, and motherhood. *Krishna* is a Christ-like figure and the 8th form (*avatar*) of *Vishnu*.

Freud expressed similar ideas in his concepts of libido, the basic life force, with two branches of *eros* (creative) and *thanatos* (destructive) forces. Jung's *archetypes* in dreams and myths are also similar to ancient Hindu ideas. The West has favored male gods. In the East, male gods and female goddesses are common. Sometimes a deity is both male and female. An ancient Hindu saying: "Male and female are as two wings of the same bird." And, in the *Bhagavad-Gita* (9.17): "I am the father of the universe. I am the mother of the universe. I am creator-of-all."

Brahma's female consort was *Saraswati*, goddess of knowledge. For *Vishnu* it was *Lakshmi*, goddess of love. There are many lesser gods such as *Indra* of the heavens and weather, *Agni* of fire, *Surya* of the sun, and *Yama* of unknown countries. Some gods are believed to have animal forms, such as the *sacred cow*. Unlike the West, there are village and family deities. This is not confusing to Hindus because all are aspects of *Brahma*. An example given to explain this is water that is the same whether it is in streams, rivers, lakes, oceans, dew, fog, rain, snow, or ice.

The **Vedas** are scriptures believed to date back more than 5000 years. It is likely they were chanted before there was writing. They are poems, prayers, hymns, and chants. The mystic *Upanishads* are included. The *Bhagavad-Gita* is a dialog between the *Krishna* and warrior *Arjuna*. *Puranas* are legends of creation, heroes and heroines, gods and goddesses. *Ramayana* is the story of good Prince *Rama* and demon *Ravana*. *Manu Smriti* describes and justifies the caste system, now illegal in India but persists in some social bias. The *Mahabharata* is a collection of stories of good and evil. The six major branches of Hindu philosophy:

1. On logic and reason (*Nyaya*)
2. On nature as guide (*Vaisheska*)
3. On creation themes *(Sankhya)*
4. On rituals (*Purva-mimansa*)
5. On the *Bhagavad-Gita*, *Upanishads*, and *Brahma Sutra (Vedanta)*.
6. On physical and meditative exercise *(Yoga)*

Yoga is a philosophy and meditative system to free a person from worldliness and karmic rebirth. The word is from the Sanskrit *yuga* which means "to yoke or to be one with" cosmic consciousness and *Brahma*. It may have been practiced before there was writing. The *Yoga Sutra* was written about 200 BCE attributed to *Patanjali*.

Yoga has eight levels, called limbs. There's an old saying: "There are eight limbs to the yoga tree and its fruit is tranquility." A man who practices it is a *yogi* and a woman a *yogini*. Belief in a personal god is not necessary, so an atheist can be a yogi or yogini. Yoga does not conflict with most religions though in the West it is most used for meditation or exercise. Those who are closer to karmic liberation are called "old souls." Gandhi was revered in this way. The eight limbs of yoga:

1. *Yama*, moral conduct, non-violent, without excess
2. *Niyama*, self control and selflessness
3. *Asana*, meditative postures
4. *Pranayama*, breath energy and control
5. *Pratyahara*, to control senses
6. *Dharana*, to focus attention
7. *Dhyana*, for meditative awareness
8. *Samadhi*, to achieve at-oneness

Siddhi are feats beyond normal made possible by yogic practice. Ancients believed they could change nature in this way. Levitation is a legendary *siddhi* never scientifically validated. However, there is evidence yogis can surpass normal body function. For example, research confirms their ability to survive in an airtight chamber beyond normal limits. Those who practice yoga report less stress and improved adaptive coping. Today therapists use biofeedback, hypnosis, and massage, examples of how modern science uses and refines ancient practices. The varieties of yoga:

Asparsha, "no-touch yoga," living a hermit life;
Bhakti, of ritual and devotions for self-control and
    selfless love of God or Nature;

Gyana, "the yoga of knowledge" to remove ignorance
by reason and "analytic will";

Hatha, a focus on body control through physical and
mental exercises;

Jhana, a focus on reality and non-reality, renouncing
what the West considers real but in yoga is unreal;

Karma, "the way of work and service" that overcomes
ego and selfishness without personal gain;

Kundalini "serpent power," psychic energy coiled at
the base of the spine that by meditation rises up
through body centers (*chakras*);

Mantra, based on chant meditation using names of
Krishna and others;

Raja or *royal yoga,* a blend of *kundalini, mantra, bhakti,
karma,* and *jhana* yoga to steady the mind.

BUDDHISM

Buddhism is a philosophy of life and a system of
character development that later became a religion. It is
remarkably consistent with current psychology. There is
no named god and for that reason some consider it to be
atheistic. Buddhism emphasizes character building and so
it can supplement most religions. Some in the East do not
find it a contradiction to be Buddhist and Christian. There
are several kinds of Buddhism:

Hinayana ("the lesser vehicle") follows the *Theravada*
tradition. It is called "lesser vehicle" or "lone rider" (*arhat*)
because it emphasizes a personal path to enlightenment
(*nirvana*). It is called the 1st turning of the *Dharma* wheel.
Dharma means body of teaching, system or dogma. Today
it is found in Burma, Sri Lanka, Thailand, Laos, and
Cambodia and

Mahayana ("the great vehicle") focuses on "insight into emptiness" (*shunyata*) and Buddhahood attained by selfless service, the *bodhisattva* ideal. It is a "greater vehicle" like a carriage form all rather than the *Theravada* lone rider. It is called the 2nd turning of the Dharma wheel. Today it is found in Vietnam, Korea, Japan, and China. *Zen Buddhism* is part of Mahayana and began as *Dhyana Buddhism* in northern India in the 2nd r 4rd century CE. *Dhyana* means wisdom. In the 5th century CE it spread to China as *Ch'an Buddhism* (*Ch'an* is Chinese for *dhyana*), then to Japan as *Zen* (Japanese for *dhyana*). .

Vajrayana ("diamond vehicle") also began in northern India then spread to Tibet and Nepal. It emphasizes study of esoteric texts (*Tantras*), rituals, mystic symbols, and yogic practices. It is called the 3rd turning of the Dharma wheel.

There have been and are many branches of Buddhism but all of them recognize and value Buddha's **Four Noble Truths** and **Noble 8-fold Path**. Buddha was born and raised Hindu but differed with the concept of karma as endless rebirths and the caste system based on it. He was born about 563 BCE in northern India, the son of Suddodhana Gautama, chief of the Sakya warrior caste. Named Gautama Siddhartha, he became known as Sakyamuni, "the sage of the Sakyas,"and finally as *Buddha*.

Much that is written about him cannot be verified. It is said a holy man prophesied to Suddodhana his son would become a great spiritual leader to relieve pain and suffering. But he wanted his son to succeed him to continue to lead the Sakyas and shielded his son from seeing any pain or suffering, providing a secure and comfortable environment. Gautama married Yasodhara.

Gautama married Yasodhara but despite a happy family life he obsessed over the meaning of life. At age 29 he happened to see four persons: one very old, another sick, a corpse, and a seemingly happy but poor hermit. He saw that living means getting old, sick, and dying – the pain and suffering predicted by the holy man when Gautama was born. Troubled by what he saw and also fascinated with the hermit who seemed serene and untroubled though impoverished, he left home in 522 BCE just before the birth of his son Rahula. Living as a hermit in the forest, he searched for "the end of suffering" which came to be referred to as *The Great Renunciation.*

He wandered for six years, studying from gurus. He almost died from fasting and the hard ascetic life and despite intense meditation and suffering he still did not found how to end suffering. Then, sitting under a bo tree he achieved *the Great Enlightenment* and became a *Buddha* (an awakened one). He saw life as based on four truths, two of suffering, two of deliverance, and an 8-fold path. Thiese became the *Dharma*, the way to enlightenment (*nirvana*) that relieves suffering and breaks the chain of karmic rebirth.

Buddha taught for the first time in the Deer Park at Benares and five hermits became followers. He called his teachings "the message from the heart" or "middle way" and said the search for spiritual truth can begin any time: "Your goal can be reached no matter where you turn, right or left. All roads lead upward and you can start anywhere." He had an amazing grasp of psychological concepts. He described the *ayatana* of sensing and perceiving: the eye for form, ear for sound, nose for smell, tongue for taste, body for touch, and mind for higher awareness.

At the time he taught this Egyptians were mummifying bodies discarding brains as useless mucus! Socrates wouldn't be born for another hundred years. 500 years before Jesus, he was teaching the *Five Precepts*: do no harm to any living thing; use no false speech; never take what is not freely given; do not drink intoxicants, avoid sensual excess or misconduct. He taught that wisdom (*prajna*) comes from free and open study of *ten subjects*, studied very carefully like grabbing a snake by its tail (great risk of being bitten):

1. Mythic tradition (*anussava*)
2. Teaching tradition (*parampura*)
3. Word-of-mouth (*itikira*)
4. Scripture (*pitakasampada*)
5. Logic (*takkahatu*)
6. Reason (*nayahatu*)
7. Validity (*akharaparavitakka*)
8. Consensual validity (*ditthinijjhakkhati*)
9. Competent teacher (*bhabbaruptata*)
10. Teacher reputation (*samano nogaru*)

THE FOUR NOBLE TRUTHS

The *Four Noble Truths* are the theory and the *8-fold path* is the practice, the *way* to *nirvana* enlightenment. Four signs of enlightenment are freedom, insight, moral purity, serene contentment and childish joy.

1st NOBLE TRUTH: THE WHEEL
(Dukkha)
Existence is painful

The *First Noble Truth* is a message of pain, that every living thing knows pain. We are born in pain, die in pain, and some life pain is inevitable. The symbol is the huge wheel of destiny on which all living things are impaled. Some life pain is inevitable. It can be physical, mental, or both. Buddha' examples of physical pain: birth, illness, hunger, thirst, injury, aging, death, accidents, catastrophes. Examples of mental pain: anger, fear, hate, frustration, anxiety, selfishness, reckless ambition, and excessive sensuality. There is psychological pain is in the seven Ds: dissatisfaction, depression, disappointment, discomfort, deprivation, distortion, and delusion (ignorance).

2nd NOBLE TRUTH: THE WHEEL'S HUB (Tanha)
The pain is within

The *Second Noble Truth* is the source of pain is within you, from what Buddha called craving or selfishness. He warned against six extremes that cause suffering, those of form, sound, smell, flavor, things, and mind-objects. They can be overcome by attention to their sources: eye, ear, nose, tongue, body, and mind. Research confirms a psychological component to pain. The longer it persists, the worse it feels because of frustration that adds to it.

3rd NOBLE TRUTH: IT NEED NOT BE SO (Nirodha)
It need not be so!

The first two truths are negative and pessimistic. The message of the *Third Noble Truth* is: it need not be so. The source of suffering and karmic rebirth can be stopped.

4th NOBLE TRUTH: THE WAY (Magga)
There is deliverance

The *Fourth Noble Truth* is "the way" from suffering, the Noble 8-fold Path, eight steps to higher awareness by study, meditation, and practice. The 8-fold path is a course in character building as timely as when first taught 2500 years ago. Buddha called it "the wide path" or "middle way open to all." The first two Noble Truths are negative: living is painful, the pain self-inflicted. The last two are positive: it need not be so, and the 8-fold path up and out. This half-dark half-light pairing is in the Yin-yang symbol of Tao. Two areas interact in a circle, separated by an S-curve. It is further described later in this chapter.

THE 8-FOLD PATH
This is the way

Buddha said: "Forging these eight links does not bring honor or fame. It is a chain that does not bind but frees. It frees you from yourself. It frees you from itself." The eight steps are taken in order. Each step depends on completing the previous one.

STEP 1: BEST UNDERSTANDING AND VIEW

This first step is the "wake up call" of the 4th Noble Truth. It begins the journey into self and the foundation for those that follow. This step should be solid, on fully realizing the Four Noble Truths. Buddha said failure to achieve this step has caused more suffering than any others. To realize this step you need to understand and have the right view of yourself, others, truth, evil, and suffering, and their causes. When you master this step it enables you know what is important and what is not, what is good and what is evil, how thoughts, feelings, words and actions can help or hinder you along the 8-fold path.

STEP 2: BEST THINKING

This step is to see what's there, not what you want to see, would like to see, or are afraid to see. It is being able to see without naming because doing so fixes and judges. Right thinking is to let everyone and everything *be* without the bias of naming or forced meaning. It is to focus on the right thing to do, what is harmless and what is harmful. Right thinking helps develop self-control. To think right is to be free of prior conditioning and preconceived notions. In Buddha's words you become "as pure as a gentle breeze."

STEP 3: BEST SPEECH

To achieve this step you need to speak truth kindly, simply, or remain silent. If you know nothing, say nothing. If you can't say or add anything good, remain silent. Do not lie or gossip. Speak or be silent unify, join together and not to separate. Use words to simplify and not complicate. Give light not heat, help, not hurt. Buddha said: "Wrong speech hurts and cannot heal." He described five kinds of wrong speech: glib talk, lies, slander, harsh words or idle chatter. Five kinds of right speech: modest, sincere, truthful, dependable, and consistent. The best speech is to agree to disagree and hold to truth without deception. It can be risky. You can be "honest to a fault." Norman Vincent Peale once commented: "Twist the truth and make a hit; tell the truth and get hit!" Buddha knew the risk when he said: "As the elephant endures the arrow so you should patiently bear with abuse, for there are many unkind archers in the world."

STEP 4: BEST ACTION AND CONDUCT

Buddha summarized this step as "every action should weaken a fault." It is to seek, enjoy, and be satisfied only with what you need, and graciously accept what is given to you. You do not take what is not yours or indulge to excess. Whatever you do should be for the good. If you can't do good, do nothing. Like Hippocrates, Buddha cautioned followers to "do no harm." It is still the legal rule of thumb in negligence cases. It is being kind and gentle, rejoicing in the happiness of others. Buddha described "defilements" to be avoided: murder, stealing, lying, slander, ill will, sexual misconduct, useless talk, harsh words, false views, covetousness, and drug abuse. He warned: "There is no fire like lust; passion does not die out, it burns out." It is said Buddha counseled his son Rahula: "As you see your reflection in a mirror, so you should reflect on what you are doing."

STEP 5: BEST LIVELIHOOD

Right livelihood is finding work that satisfies and fulfills, to realize that life is as much a mission as a career to be content with what you do for a living and satisfied doing it.   Buddha urged followers to "find a pure livelihood" without dealing in lethal weapons, poisons, intoxicants, animals for slaughter, or anything that hurts people. He cautioned against killing, stealing, cheating, dishonesty, and deceit.

STEP 6: BEST EFFORT

This step is being able to do your best wherever you are, whatever you're doing. Buddha said: "There is nothing of such power to prevent evil as right effort." He described four great efforts: to avoid craving and ignorance, overcome them "so they have no hold on you," develop energy and strength to do good and avoid evil, and to continue along the 8-fold path. His advice: "As weeds are removed before seed is sown, so you should remove unwanted weeds from your mental garden."

STEP 7: BEST MINDFULNESS

Right mindfulness is to be aware and attentive, "with it," and able to focus attention. It involves critical judgment, a higher level than Step 1 understanding. It is being able to think what you choose to think and what is important to enlightenment. Mindfulness should be a daily practice in word and action. Then it then becomes like a trusted friend always at your side. A sign of this step is a quick mind, what Buddha described as "being heedful among the heedless, awake among those asleep, and so the wise succeed like a fast horse that overtakes a slower one." It is having reverence for all life, a view that every living thing has a purpose, and all men, women, and children are in the same family.

STEP 8: BEST CONCENTRATION

Buddha said completing the 8-fold path is like making a strong rope of intertwined strands of Steps 6, 7, and 8. These three last steps interact in synergy, greater than the sum of the parts. Buddha saw right concentration as the way to develop the mind and character. Meditation is not to transcend existence as in yoga but to focus on mental processes and overcome them. The result is a calm, reflective state of mind "beyond bliss and suffering when the mind is pure and radiant as at birth." Buddha: "The unwise are half-filled vessels. The wise are deep, calm lakes."

Buddha taught two ways to concentrate: steady mind (*samatha-bhavana*) of inner peace, and insight meditation (*vipassana-bhavana*), of oneness or mystic unity. Insight meditation frees the mind to wander freely, emptying itself of needless thoughts, and expanding consciousness. Mountain men in the old West said that if you're ever lost in a snowstorm let go of the reins and your horse will take you home. Insight meditation is like that. Zen Buddhists call it "falling off an imaginary log" or "going down the well." In ancient times, Zen archers would meditate so archer, bow, arrow, and target were one. Expert marksmen today do the same, though they may be unaware Buddha it 2500 years ago

BUDDHA'S LAST WORDS

Buddha's "message from the heart" radiates in his final words. He was 80 and had traveled widely to explain the four noble truths and 8-fold path. From the accounts of his death it is likely he died of food poisoning or acute indigestion and he knew he was dying. It is said hundreds of monks and nuns were with him at the time. They listened carefully to his last words:

Be islands unto yourselves. Be a refuge to yourselves.
See truth as an island and as a refuge. Do not seek
    a refuge in anyone but yourselves.
Who, now or after I am gone, are islands and
    refuges to themselves, and take no other
    refuge but truth as an island and refuge,
    will reach the farther shore, but they must
    make the effort themselves.
My age is now full ripe. My life draws to a close.
    I leave you. I depart, relying on myself alone.
Be earnest, then, holy, full of careful thought,
    steadfast in resolve, and watch over your own
    hearts.
Who wearies not but holds fast to his truth and
    law will cross the sea of life and bring an end
    to grief.

Do not weep. Do not distress yourselves.
　　Have I not told you it is in the very nature
　　of things we must eventually be parted from
　　all that is near and dear to us? Everything
　　born, developed, and organized has within
　　it the means of its own demise. How then
　　can it be otherwise than a being should pass
　　away? Nothing else is possible.
It may be some of you will say "the word of the
　　teacher is no more, now we are without a
　　leader." You must not think this. The Dharma
　　and Rules I have given you, let them be your
　　teacher after I am gone.
This I tell you: decay is inherent in all things.
Work out your own salvation, with diligence.

EXERCISE 8. *Some see Buddhism as more a philosophy or psychological system than a religion and follow it at the same time being Christians, Jews, or Muslims. Can you apply it in this way? Its spiritual light is non-denominational.*

ZEN: INSIGHT IN SPARKS AND FLASHES

Zen Buddhism is a method of direct insight learning that blends *Buddhism* and *Taoism*. It is about 1500 years old. A Rinzai Zen saying sums it up well: "Do not get entangled with any object but stand above, move on, and be free." According to legend Bodhidharma, "the blue-eyed monk" traveled from India to China in 520 CE and founded *Ch'an Buddhism* (pronounced like "John"). In India it was *Dhyana Buddhism* (Sanskrit *dhyana* means "meditative mind"). When it spread to Japan it became

Zen and branched into *Rinzai* (Eisai ca. 1100 CE) using *koan* riddles and meditation, and *Soto* (Dogen ca 1200 CE) that emphasized sitting meditation (*sanzen*) and readings.

In Ch'an/Zen there is no need to name anything. The world is seen as is without naming, owning, changing, or explaining it. In many ways it is the opposite of Western thought. It disagrees with Tennyson's poem "flower in the crannied wall I pluck thee from the crannies" which kills the flower for selfish enjoyment. The Zen way is to leave the flower untouched, alive, its beauty intact even if no one else saw it.

Zen "no mind" is like a clear pane of glass compared to Western mind which is more like a mirror. Zen mind sees with a third eye and hears with a third ear. It never judges. The West names, types, labels, and judges. Compared to Zen, it misses the point: ultimate reality! In Zen there is no need to add words to what exists. You already know all you need to know and very likely you know too much. The Zen goal is a free mind "open as the sky" to empty it so it becomes "no mind." Traditional learning is not *the way*. Zen is inductive, intuitive, and may seem anti-intellectual.

Zen is caught not taught, in flashes of insight called *satori* (Japanese) or *tun-wu* (Chinese). The flash (a divine spark?) can be a gentle nudge or lightning bolt impact. Paradox is often used to teach a full mind is closed to truth and must be emptied to be filled. To generate the satori flash Zen language is sometimes crude, shocking, or even profane. It can be abstract, like the student who asked a Zen master if it was wise to study scripture. The master replied: "There are no paths to the mountain. The mountain is always there. Regardless of which direction you take, you may have a very fine walk."

KOANS

Koans (*kung-an* in Chinese) are riddles to trigger a flash of insight. They can't be solved by factual knowledge. The best answers aim at meditative awareness, a mystic leap. Here's a sample *koan* dialog between master and student:

STUDENT: What is perfect enlightenment like?

MASTER: It is like thieves breaking into a vacant house.

This interaction relates to the saying "an enlightened mind is wide open as the sky," meaning empty of trivia, free of useless facts *like a vacant house!* Here are *koans* that have generated "satori sparks" for centuries. Use them to help you develop meditative awareness. Try reading one a day or typing or writing each on an index card and drawing them at random.

"SIMPLE" QUESTIONS
1. What time is it?
2. How well do you see?
3. When is your birthday? How old are you?
4. How rich are you?
5. Who is your mother?
6. Who is your teacher?
7. How much baggage do you carry?
8. What do you own?
9. Where is home?

BEST-MOST-WORST
10. Who is the best teacher?
11. What is the best knowledge?

12. Who is the best friend?
13. How can you know the most beautiful?
14. Who is your worst enemy?
15. What is the worst that could happen?

OPPOSITES
16. What is the sound of silence?
17. How is failure success?
18. How is loneliness good?
19. When is leaving arriving?
20. How is ugly beautiful?
21. How is dark light?
22. How is evil good?
23. How is sunrise sunset?
24. How are differences the same?
25. How can great be small?
26. How is empty full?
27. How is ending beginning?
28. When is a man not a man and woman not a woman? woman? When is a man a woman, a woman a man?

KOANS WITH A LESSON
29. What is the value of emptiness?
30. What is a lesson of uncarved wood?
31. What is a lesson from a seed? A flower?
32. What is a lesson from sunrise? Sunset? Noon?
33. What is a lesson from a waterfall?
34. What is a lesson from water? From the ocean? The beach?
35. What is a lesson from the wind? From the sky? From clouds?
36. What is a lesson from an insect? From a bird? From an animal?

37. What is a lesson from the earth? From the sun? From the Moon? From stars?
38. How is a baby your grandparent? And so?
39. What effect would it have if a rose was called a weed? And so?
40. How is this a happy message: Grandfather dies; father dies; son dies? And so?
41. Candle, wick, and flame, which is more important? How are they the same? And so?
42. Why give a lighted candle or lantern to a blind person? And so?
43. How can you reach higher up on tiptoe from the highest mountain? And so?
44. Two persons argue. Both are right. Neither is right. One is wrong. They teach each other but fail the lesson. How can all this be? And so?
45. A boat sinks. Does water flow into it or does it lower itself into the water? Which is more powerful? Which wins? And so?
46. How are black and white the same? Do they need each other? Which is more important?
47. Hammer hits nail. Which is more powerful, Stronger? How are they similar? How are they different? Which yields more? Which wins? And so?
48. There is a deadly snake and a piece of rope the same length and thickness in a totally dark room with no light or windows. How can you tell the snake from the rope? And so?
49. What is the sound of one hand clapping? And so?
50. Call this a sentence and you are trapped by its name. If you don't you contradict fact. So then, what do you call it? And so?

51. Explain this. Zen is nothing. Zen isn't nothing.
    Zen isn't know-thing. Zen knows. Zen no's.
    Zen nose. Zen knows nothing. Zen knows no-thing.
    Zen is something. Zen is anything. What is, is Zen
    but Zen isn't just it. Zen is but isn't.
52. Half of Zen is nonsense. Half of Zen is good sense.
    Half of Zen is both. Half of Zen is neither. How can
    this be? And so?
53. How can you play the solid iron flute that has
    no holes?

PARABLES

Parables are stories with an underlying thought or moral. They are used in Zen like *koans*, to trigger *satori*.

THE OLD MONK'S CHAIR

Buddhist monks were seated for meals by seniority. A new student sat in the chair of the oldest monk. The old monk confronted the seated student:
OLD MONK: How old are you in the Buddhist way?
STUDENT: I am as old as the prehistoric Buddha.
  (With this remark the dining room became silent
    because the student posed a powerful Zen argument)
OLD MONK: Well then move over. You are my great
    grandson.
Satori spark: This is "Zen one upsmanship" with mystic meaning in what seems a prank. Zen people are cheerful and childlike, their approach simple and selfless. Zen mind is ageless as the old monk's reply showed.

ZEN TEACUP

A scholar from the West visited a Zen Master. He told the old master he had only a short time but was eager "to learn all about Zen." The old man served the scholar tea, carefully pouring it but he kept pouring it until the cup overflowed. Shocked, the scholar exclaimed: "Can't you see it's full?" The old master smiled and replied calmly: "Just as your mind is filled and overflowing with its own ideas. I cannot pour out Zen to you unless you bring me an empty cup."

Satori spark: You can learn *about* Zen but never *know* it, *read* but never *realize* it. This interaction shows how "book learning" is of little use in experiencing Zen. The key word is to *experience* it.

ZEN MIRACLES

A Zen monk sat meditating as a Western missionary approached.

MISSIONARY: The founder of my religion could
    perform miracles. He could walk on water. What
    can you do?

ZEN MONK: I only do small miracles. When hungry I eat.
    When thirsty I drink. When lonely I think on deeper
    truths. When I am insulted I forgive.

Satori spark: Contrasts reactive West with reflective East.

SACRED MISSION

Tetsugen was a Buddhist monk in Japan. At the time there were no Buddhist scriptures in Japanese. Tetsugen made it his life mission. He went from village to village to raise the money needed. After 10 years he had enough, but the Uji River flooded and he used the money to buy rice for the hungry. He began again, traveling far and wide to raise money. After another 10 years he had enough, but there was a great plague and he used the money to buy medicine for the sick. A third time he traveled to raise money and after another 10 years he had enough. Old and tired, he saw his mission fulfilled before he died. Buddhist scriptures were printed in Japanese. They can be seen in museums and libraries today. But it is said by those who know they are not as good as his first and second editions.

Satori spark: This is similar to Leigh Hunt's poem *Abou Ben Adhem,* to whom an angel appeared "writing the names of those who loved the Lord." Abou was shocked his name was not there and said: "Then write me as one who loves his fellow man." The poem ends: "The angel did so and lo, Ben Adhem's name led all the rest." Helping others far surpassed Tetsugen's original mission.

DISCOVERING HEAVEN AND HELL

The Emperor's Captain of the Guard was a famous Samurai warrior. He retired and wanted to learn more about life and its meaning. He went to a Zen master to ask to study with him.

OFFICER: I would like to learn about philosophy
    and meditation.

ZEN MASTER: What do you want to know?

OFFICER: I want to know if there is heaven and hell.

ZEN MASTER: Who are you?

OFFICER: I was Captain of the Emperor's guard.

ZEN MASTER: Nonsense! What kind of emperor
    would have anyone like you?

OFFICER (*indignant*): I am Samurai and have won
    many battles.

ZEN MASTER: I don't believe it. You look like a
    common ignorant beggar.

   (You don't talk like that to a Samurai if you value
    your life. The officer rattled his sword, eyes blazing)

ZEN MASTER: Oh, I see you have a sword. You
    probably stole it. I doubt you know how to use
    it. It's probably rusty and too dull to cut
    anything anyway.
(That did it! The enraged officer drew his sword and
held it in both hands over the old master's head. When
a Samurai drew a sword it was always to use it)
ZEN MASTER (*calmly*): Now my son, you have half the
    answer. The gates of hell are open to you.
(Suddenly aware of his rage and its potential, in a flash
of satori insight, he dropped the sword and fell to his
knees weeping)
ZEN MASTER (*again calmly*): And now my son, the gates
    of heaven are open to you. There is no need to study
    more. Go in peace.
Satori spark: Stressful situations are often used to reflect
Zen principles. The Zen master entered the officer's world
to get his attention then provoke conflict and use it to
awaken awareness and help him achieve satori.

HEADLESS PRINCESS
    There was a princess who was very upset because
she couldn't see her head, true since eyes only look out.
Her family reassured her they could see her head but she
couldn't accept it: "You just say that because you're my
family." A mirror was placed before her but she said:
"This is just a picture of me and not my head." Her father
tied her to a post in the village square with a sign asking
all who passed to reassure her she had a head. Many did
so, but it upset her even more: "I can't see what you see. I
have no head." An old man walking slowly with a cane
read the note. He suddenly swung his cane up and struck
the princess on the top of her head. She cried out in pain.

"That," the old man said calmly, "is your head."

Satori spark: This is "tough love satori." Actions can speak louder than words and a simple direct act can be better than a wordy explanation.

FORBIDDEN WOMAN

Two Buddhist monks went begging for food in the village, a daily task. It was the rainy season and streets were muddy. A pretty girl in fine silk stood, afraid to cross the street. The first monk offered to help her. She allowed him to pick her up and carry her across the street. This upset the other monk who harangued his brother monk on the long walk back to the temple: "You know contact with women is forbidden. We should never go anywhere near a woman, let alone touch one." At the temple gate the first monk calmly said: "My brother, I put that lady down hours ago but you still carry her."

Satori spark: Zen masters often ask new arrivals: "How much baggage do you carry?" Or: "I hope you have not brought too much baggage. It takes time to dispose of it." These are Zen ways of referring to mental unfinished business, unsolved problems, and ties to the past.

EXERCISE 9. *Some call Zen anti-intellectual, but its method is to question all reality. In this way it helps free the mind of bias and unrealistic expectations. It can be an enlightening leap to higher consciousness. Think of how you can use it in your everyday life to take a stimulating mystic leap.*

TAO
TRANSCENDENT TRUTH

Psychologist Abraham Maslow and psychiatrist Carl Jung found Eastern philosophies relevant to personality development. Both referred to Taoist (pronounced *dow-ist*) concepts. The classic text is the *Tao Teh Ching* or *Book of Tao* (say "dow"). It is one of the most translated Chinese classics. The author is thought to be *LaoTse* (say "louts") or *LaoTzu* ("louts-zoo"). The name means "old man." He lived in China in the 5th century BCE), at about the same time Buddha was living in northern India ad K'ung FuTse (Confucius) was living in China but a different province.

One legend says LaoTse was keeper of the archives of China (unlikely) and "the wisest man in China. It is said that when he was 80 or 90 he left his work behind and rode an ox or donkey to the mountains to die. The guard at the frontier recognized him and refused to let him pass because he had not left his great wisdom for posterity. The old man sat and wrote the 81 sutras (from Sanskrit *sutram* meaning strand of thought) that has become the *Book of Tao*. He left it with the guard, then rode away. LaoTse's legendary modest clothing, few possessions, humble way of travel, and going to the mountain symbolize Taoist and Zen values.

As for the name *Tao Teh Ching*, *Tao* cannot be defined in words. Like God, it is too great an idea for words. *Teh* (say "duh") is the highest human virtue. *Ching* (say "jing") means book. It was written about 500 BCE but was probably taught or chanted before writing and as early as 3000 BCE. In ancient China there were no books, but scrolls or bundles of painted bamboo sticks. The 81 sutras in current translations are not in logical order or internally consistent. This is likely due to the scrolls and sticks being mixed over time. The sutras that follow are in two groups: those about *Tao* and those about *Teh*. A line may be moved for continuity. There are some wording changes such as *wise* for *sage* or *wise man* to remove gender bias which is inconsistent with "the way of Tao." Each sutra ends with its traditional number in parentheses. Not all 81 sutras are included, only those that directly relate to *Tao* and *Teh*.

SUTRAS ABOUT TAO

TAO IS NAMELESS

The Tao described in words is not the real Tao. Words cannot describe it. It is the unnamed source of creation. Named, it is the Great Mother of everything. To see Tao the observer must be motiveless. An observer with selfish motives sees only the surface not inside. Both observers differ in the depth of their observations. Both observers are similar because they are both human. Within humanity is the key to open the door of creation *(Sutra 1)*

TAO IS ABSOLUTE

There is something mysterious, without beginning, without end, that existed before the heavens and the earth. It is unmoving, infinite, independent, never changing. It is everywhere and it is inexhaustible. It is the great mother of everything. I do not know its name. If I must name it I call it Tao and recognize it as supreme. Supreme means unending. Unending means far-reaching. Far-reaching means eventually returning. Tao is supreme, the universe is supreme, earth is supreme, and humanity is supreme. There are four supremes and humanity is one of them.

Humanity is subject to the laws of the earth. The earth is subject to the laws of the universe. The universe is subject to the laws of Tao. Tao is subject to the laws of its own nature (*Sutra 25*).

EXISTENCE, NON-EXISTENCE

Looked for it cannot be seen; it is invisible. Listened for it cannot be heard; it is inaudible. Reached for it cannot be touched; it is intangible. These three are beyond analysis yet they are one. Tao rises like the sun but it does not illuminate. Tao sets like the sun but does not darken. It is without beginning, without end, infinite, indefinable. It is the form of the formless, existence in non-existence, the greatest mystery. Meet it and it has no face. Follow it and it has no back. Hold close to timeless Tao to master your own existence. Knowing what is now you can know what has been. This is a clue to Tao (*Sutra 14*).

VITAL NON-EXISTENCE

Thirty spokes join at the hub but the use of the wheel depends on the place where nothing exists. Clay is molded into a vase but its ultimate use depends on the space where nothing exists. Doors and windows are built into the walls of a house but their use depends on the spaces where nothing exists. So, there is an advantage in using what can be seen, what exists, and there is an advantage in using what cannot be seen, what is non-existent (*Sutra 11*).

SAME-DIFFERENT

Tao is like a drawn bow. The highest part is lowered, the lowest part raised, overall length is shortened, and overall depth is lengthened. Tao lowers the highest and raises the lowest but the worldly way pushed up the high and puts down the low. Who can take from the high and give to the low? Followers of Tao give without receiving and receive without giving *(Sutra 77)*.

SUTRAS ABOUT TEH

TAO AND TEH

Tao causes everything to exist and Teh sustains them. Reality shapes everything and fate finishes them. Thus, everything has Tao and Teh naturally. Through Tao and Teh there is growth, security, and support. Everything exists through Tao. Nothing is rejected. Everything is achieved through Teh. Nothing fails. And yet, Tao and The are not possessive and do not interfere *(Sutra 51)*.

TEH OF THE ANCIENTS

Ancient followers of Tao were wise, subtle, profound, so deeply understanding they themselves were not understood. It is important, then, to describe them: cautious, like crossing a stream in midwinter; observant, like moving through a strange land; modest, yielding like melting ice; dignified as honored guests; genuine as un- carved wood; receptive as an open valley; as friendly as muddy water freely mixing. Who can make sense of a world as clouded as muddy water? Left alone it clears itself. Can this clarity and calm remain? Move hastily and it will cloud up again. Can there be movement without clouding? Those with Tao do so, moving ahead unselfishly and caringly, as unselfish as a tiny seedling that grows gently, thrives and ripens *(Sutra 15)*.

REAL WEALTH

To have the world know of you, or to know yourself, which is more important? Which is more valuable, money or your mind? Which can lead to the greater evil, winning or losing? Excess leads to loss. Great wealth invites wrong-doing. Being content prevents harmful extremes. Knowing when to stop prevents danger. To know this is to endure (*Sutra 44*).

WATER POWER

There is nothing weaker or more yielding than water yet it wears down the hard and strong. There is nothing quite like it. In the same way, the weak can overcome the strong and the flexible can overcome the rigid. Anyone can see this but few put it to use. So, the wise know straight words can seem crooked. They know whoever bears the shame of a nation is fit to lead that nation and whoever bears the sins of the world is fit to lead the world (*Sutra 78*).

STRAIGHT TALK

Nature is sparing in its talk. High winds seldom last the whole morning. Heavy rain seldom lasts the whole day. Where do these originate? In nature and if nature is so sparing in its talk how much more should you be? Who follows Tao is like Tao. Who follows Teh has Teh. Who abandons Tao and Teh will be abandoned by Tao and Teh. Who seeks Tao and Teh will be welcomed by Tao and Teh. Who seeks abandonment will be welcomed by abandonment (*Sutra 23*).

EASY DOES IT

What does not move can be easily grasped. What has not yet happened can be planned more easily. What is rigid can be easily broken. What is tiny can be easily dispersed. Cope with problems before they grow. Exert control before there is confusion. A tree with an arm's girth of trunk grows from a tiny sprout. A nine-storied terrace rises from a clump of dirt. A journey of a thousand miles begins with the first step. Action can spoil. Over-reaching can lose. The truly wise are not active so they do not spoil anything. They do not reach far so they do not lose Things are often spoiled very near successful completion. Be as careful at the end as you were at the beginning. The truly wise want the unwanted and do not value what is rare. They study what is unstudied and preserve what is lost. They help the course of nature and never interfere with it *(Sutra 64)*.

UNDERSTANDING MISUNDERSTANDING

These teachings are easily understood and readily put into practice yet they are not understood and not practiced. Words have specific meanings and actions have specific purposes. I am not so specific and so people do not understand me. I understand being misunderstood. The true knowledge of that understanding is mine. The truly wise wear common clothes. They carry their jewels in their hearts (*Sutra 70*).

THE BEST LEADERSHIP

Lead as you would cook a small fish: do not overdo it. Lead with Tao and evil fades. Evil continues but will not be harmful. As evil ceases to be harmful leaders cease to be harmful. Then both leader and people have Teh *(Sutra 60)*.

LESS IS MORE

Scholars seek to know more and more every day. The followers of Tao need to know less and less every day. Lessen factual knowledge and serenity is within reach.

With serenity everything can be accomplished. The world belongs to those who let go of it. Try to own it and it is already beyond reach *(Sutra 48)*.

AVOID RISK

Stand on tiptoe and you are unsteady. Walk with long strides and you cannot long keep up the pace. Make a show of yourself and you cannot shine. Be self righteous and you lose respect. If you are self centered you cannot be loved by others. If you seek personal gain you cannot be a true leader. According to the Tao these attitudes are excessive and unnecessary. They should be avoided, even in personal matters. Therefore, followers of Tao avoid them *(Sutra 24)*.

FLEXIBLE STRENGTH

What is living is soft and yielding. What is dead is hard and unyielding. Living animals and plants are soft and pliant. Dead, they are withered and brittle. Being rigid and unyielding is to be like death. Being flexible and yielding is to be alive. A headstrong army will lose in battle like an unyielding tree snapping under the axe. The place of the strong is below. The place of the gentle is above *(Sutra 76)*.

LOWLY HIGHER LEADERSHIP

How do oceans and rivers have dominion over the land? It is because they lower themselves. To be elevated by people, lower yourself to them. To lead, walk among

them. Thus the truly wise are above but people do not feel their weight. When they walk in front people do not feel blocked. The whole world respects and never tires of such leadership. Because the truly wise are not quarrelsome no one quarrels with them *(Sutra 66)*.

MEANINGFUL DIFFERENCES

To appreciate what is beautiful one must know about ugliness, its opposite. To know what is good one must know about evil, it's opposite. So, perception involves differences: reality and fantasy are differing thoughts; difficult and easy are differing efforts; far and near are differing distances; high and low are differing heights; shrill and deep are differing tones; before and after are differing times. The truly wise accept this and work diligently despite differences or quibbling over words. They teach by example and not by words alone. They are genuinely helpful and they do not discriminate. They are positive and not possessive. They do not proclaim their importance and so their achievements shine and can never be dimmed *(Sutra 2)*.

EXTREME DANGER

There is danger in extremes. Pull a bowstring too far and you wish you had let go before. Hone a sword's blade too well and it will wear too soon. Fill your house with gold and jade and you invite thieves. Be arrogant and proud and you prepare for your own downfall. When you reach your goal be satisfied to go no further. That is the Way of Tao *(Sutra 9)*.

MYSTIC YIN-YANG

Know the Mystic Father Yang and Mystic Mother Yin and you are like a valley receptive to everything. You have the Teh of an innocent child. Being aware of Yang light but also Yin darkness is to know the noble standard and you have absolute Teh. Becoming famous but remaining humble is to be like a valley so vast it can hold the whole world. You have the Teh of Mystic Unity. Divide the unity and its parts are tools. In the hands of the truly wise they are means to an end but never an end themselves (*Sutra 28*).

LAST WORDS OF LAO-TSE?

We have no record of any last words of LaoTse, but *Sutra 67* is likely what he might have said:

I leave you three jewels. Guard them and keep them safe. The first is love, to know living is giving, everyone is your brother or sister, and the one great law of life is love. Without love, nothing is possible. The second is moderation, to know the mystic balance, avoid extremes, and accept differences as a way to grow. The third is humility, to know you are born with nothing and will die with nothing, but to die and be remembered is to have immortality.

EXERCISE 10. *Taoism has been called a nature philosophy. Though it became a religion and is still practiced, the sutras are non-denominational and compatible with the world's major religions. Use them to help appreciate the beauty of nature. Truth itself has this elegant aspect.*

K'UNG FU-TSE (Confucius)

K'ung FuTse was Latinized by western writers to **Confucius**. He lived in China 551-479 BCE, the same time as LaoTse but in a different province. There is no evidence they ever met but one legend describes what might have happened. Hearing of LaoTse's great wisdom, K'ung FuTse sent a messenger to invite him to visit. As the messenger passed beyond the horizon another figure appeared, an old man on a donkey: LaoTse!

K'ung FuTse relied on formal knowledge but LaoTse knew by mystic awareness. According to the legend, K'ung FuTse greeted his guest and proudly showed him his large library. He was moved when LaoTse said: "It is good. Very useful." Delighted, K'ung FuTse said he spent many hours reading. "Yes," LaoTse agreed, "in winter books can be burned to keep you warm." The legend contrasts factual knowledge with mystic intuition and with a typical Zen stinger.

Buddha, LaoTse, and K'ung FuTse reflect three major aspects of Asian thought: Buddha, for personal growth and character building in the *Four Noble Truths* and *8-fold path*; LaoTse for the intuitive wisdom in the Book of Tao (Zen blended Taoism with Buddhism); K'ung FuTse (Confucius) for the social order described in *The Analects*.

EXERCISE 11. *When you feel you understand this chapter well enough to form an opinion, ask yourself and reflect on how "Eastern" you are in your life, work, and spiritual awareness. Both Western and Eastern religions seek to improve spirituality, but why not use the ideas of both in your spiritual development?*

SI SPARKS

31. There is the authoritative instant and the moment of freedom and they are always killing each other (Carl Sandburg, in *The people, yes*)

32. The superior do not set mind for or against anything, but do what is right (K'ung FuTse, *Analects* 4:10).
33. Superior people seek what is within themselves. Inferior people seek what is in others (Kung FuTse, *Analects* 15:20).
34. Perfect virtue is to everywhere practice five traits: depth, kindness, sincerity, benevolence, and earnestness (Kung FuTse, *Analects* 17:6).
35. Quit this world. Quit the next world. Then quit quitting (Zen saying).
36. Cherish what is within you, avoid what is without; excess knowledge is a curse (ChuangTse, 369-286 BCE, *On tolerance*).
37. Great people are those who never lose their child-heart (Mencius, 372-289 BCE, *Book IV*, 2:12).
38. The Great Beginning first created emptiness. Emptiness created the universe. Essences of heaven and earth became Yin and Yang. Essences of Yin and yang became the seasons. Essences of seasons became all the living things in the world (Huai NanTse, 2nd century BCE).
39. The world of suchness is void and empty because it teases the mind out of thought dumbfounding the chatter of definition so there's nothing left to be said yet we are not confronted with literal nothingness (Alan Watts, *The way of Zen*).
40. The map is not the territory. Don't push the river (Zen sayings).

5

SI IN THE SCIENCES

> Religion that does not
> touch science, and science
> that does not touch religion,
> are mutilated and barren.
> -- William Inge (1860-1954)

Moral conduct, a goal of religion, is mainly external and in social behavior. It is learned, not a genetic trait. SI is internal, personal, and a genetic gift that can be further developed individually. Religion is shared, in a named group identity, as if one wears the uniform of a specific organization. It is formal and with a fixed code of conduct. Religion is like studying details of a moral microcosm with a mental microscope. SI is more like using a telescope to explore the macrocosm, transcend details, and expand consciousness. It moves toward mystic unity with the universe, a cosmic consciousness.

Giuseppe Mazzini (1805-1872 CE) wrote of an ideal blend of these two approaches: "Every religion sets before mankind a new educational idea, a fragment of eternal truth that becomes part of universal tradition, as mountain climber reaching high ground sees another summit above" (Beck, 1968).

Being religious and being spiritual are not the same. An atheist can be spiritual but not religious. Many who attend church or temple are religious by definition, but not necessarily spiritual. Here's how they compare:

RELIGION	SI
social	personal
organizational	individual
denominational	universal
group identity	mystic unity
structured	unstructured
defined path	undefined path
shared goals	personal experience
conduct focus	mental process focus
formal ritual	personal meditation
scripture-based	spirit-based
revolutionary	evolutionary

SI joins religion with science, an uncomfortable union because of mutual distrust. Religion and science have been blinded, seeing only their own mission and goals. Each uses its own methods, language, books, and journals. SI touches both and all the sub-specialties. There are many flags, many defended territories. This has been obvious to writers outside religion and science. Pearl Buck saw science and religion as "two sides of the same glass through which we see darkly until the two, focusing together, reveal the truth." Those within science have become aware of drowning in trivia. Robert Sternberg, a major personality and intelligence theorist, sees psychology as "increasingly fragmented" and recommends any subject should be studied "from a variety of different perspectives."

Philosophers have had similar views. Bertrand Russell called for a "calmly dispassionate science capable of that union with the universe that constitutes its highest good." Some in religion have welcomed such a science. William

Inge, a Cambridge University divinity professor, wrote: "A spiritual interpretation of the world is a psycho- logical necessity from which we cannot escape and an avenue to objective truth."

To arrive at truth, both science and religion need to be more open, to each other and to truth regardless of its source. Julian Huxley urged religion "to abandon its claims to fixity and certitude since the pursuit of truth is essentially sacred." For science, he saw "a religious aspect," since truth is sacred regardless of its source. Martin Luther King Jr. said: "Science deals mainly with facts; religion deals mainly with values. The two are not rivals. They are complementary" (Frank, 1999).

Debate over divine creation and natural evolution has been a major obstacle to science and religion becoming partners in the search for truth. Teilhard's *hominization to omega* provides an ideal bridge. Allport had much the same idea: "The mind is still growing, stretching its rational capacities as far as it can with the logic of induction, deduction, a weighing of probabilities, and what is also metaphysically true, outer revelation and mystical experience that provide supernatural assurance."

There are encouraging signs of sharing across differences. *Dynamical systems theory* or *complexity theory* includes input from economics, ecology, mathematics, physics, philosophy, psychology, computer science, and linguistics. It evolved from *information processing theory*, artificial intelligence, virtual reality, and chaos theory. Another new movement is *evolutionary psychology*. It welcomes ethologists and zoologists to explore the genetic basis of behavior. SI is compatible with all these movements.

EXERCISE 12. *Do you see how science and religion differ in their approach to finding truth? Which do you prefer? Choose either and you admit to a bias. Do you see the value of being open to truth regardless of its source?*

SI IN THE BEHAVIORAL SCIENCES

Psychology is the science of behavior and mental processes but it is reluctant to accept spiritual intelligence. Even Howard Gardner who originally spoke and wrote about it later called it "problematic." In a 2000 journal article he wrote: "existential intelligence captures at least in part what individuals mean when they speak of spirit-concerns." He saw existentialism as a better fit because it includes "a desire to know about experiences and cosmic entities not readily apprehended in a material sense." Spirituality and existentialism are strange bedfellows, indeed.

In the same article, Gardner conceded "spirituality is worthy of study as an intelligence if that lens illuminates its nature." It most certainly does! His resistance to SI reflects some frustration: "I cannot enumerate how often I have been said to posit a 'spiritual intelligence' though I have never done so and have in fact explicitly rejected that possibility both orally and in writing." Perhaps his change of opinion was the result of overzealous educators too quick to apply it to school curricula before it could be clearly defined and demonstrated.

Science is conservative and slow to accept anything not clearly proven. SI is a mental process more than a behavior pattern and therefore difficult to study. Gardner accepted this reality: "The world of the naturalist seems straight-forward. In contrast, even a hesitant entry into the world of spirituality reveals a far more complex picture." And: "The majority of scholars in cognitive and behavioral sciences turn away from questions of a spiritual nature, consigning this realm to true believers and quacks." He considered existential intelligence "the most un-ambiguously cognitive strand of the spiritual." His bias is obvious in characterizing "spiritual nature" as a realm of true believers and quacks," his choice of words *cognitive* and *behavioral* reflecting psychology's perceptual set of more head than heart, and forcing spirituality into the dubious area of existentialism.

Gardner listed eight criteria needed to validate any type of intelligence, providing an opportunity to rebut his argument. Here's how spiritual intelligence satisfies his eight criteria:

1. Isolation by brain damage. Choosing brain damage as a more valid criterion of intelligence than healthy brain function is unusual. It would seem healthy brain function would be preferable. There is evidence of SI in the healthy brain. *Neurotheology* is a new field of study of brain function in religious and spiritual experiences. *Newsweek* focused on it in an entire issue May 7, 2001 entitled: *"God and the brain: How we're wired for spirituality."*I referred to the 1997 conference of the *Society for Neuroscience* where neurologist Vilayanur Ramachandran said: "There is a neural basis for religious experience."

The *Newsweek* articles described research using brain-imaging instruments to measure meditation. In one experiment Franciscan nuns and Tibetan Buddhists were studied as they meditated. At first, frontal lobes were active, suggesting focused attention. Slowly, areas of the awake state and fight-flight weakened. The brain's right hemisphere became more active suggesting a change in reality testing.

Other researchers, using PET and SPECT instruments, have found what they call a "spirituality circuit." When meditating, parietal lobe activity is low. That is the area involved in self-perception and orientation. Input from the hippocampus to the parietal lobes decreases as temporal lobe activity increases. Feelings of awe and ecstasy occur when the middle temporal lobe is active. Its lower lobe involves emotion with visual imagery. This helps explain visions and voices some believe are divine. Michael Persinger at Canada's Laurentian University got similar results using a weak magnetic field to the temporal area.

In 1998, Newberg and d'Aquili described what they called "religiogenic brain mechanisms," circuits from the cortex to the limbic and autonomic nervous systems. The left inferior parietal lobe stimulates frontal lobes, mostly in the left hemisphere. This was called the "cognitive operator" since it is without sense input. The research showed that if there is no apparent cause for an event "gods, powers, spirits, or some other causative construct can be formed by the cognitive operator."

This research also found a "holistic operator" that "permits reality to be viewed as a whole or gestalt into a larger contextual framework." It arises in the non-dominant parietal lobe near logic and language areas of the dominant hemisphere. The left parietal lobe is involved in simplistic thought and the right side by abstract and holistic thought.

Research confirms spiritual experiences involve five kinds of autonomic stimulation:

(a) High parasympathetic arousal to "extraordinary states of quiescence" such as in meditation, prayer, or ritual.

(b) High sympathetic arousal by deep concentration and focused attention that block other thoughts or sensations.

(c) A parasympathetic trance-like state with spillover into the sympathetic causing a flash, high, or rush. Is this what happened to St. Paul on the road to Damascus?

(d) A sympathetic ecstatic high with vivid hallucination and spillover into a rebound trancelike state in the parasympathetic. This may be what happens when people have visions.

(e) High arousal of parasympathetic and sympathetic at the same time. This causes a "total breakdown" such as in a mystical or spiritual experience. Sense of time and self-object boundaries are disrupted. Examples: near-death experiences (NDE) ; dramatic religious conversion.

These and other studies are evidence of specific brain activity during spiritual experiences. Science explains it as a neurochemical process perceived by some as spiritual. Religion sees it as evidence of a spiritual consciousness. Both agree there is brain activity but differ as to what it means. It's as if science described the Mona Lisa as only an arrangement of paints, the Taj Mahal as just another building design, Shakespeare's plays as groups of words, and Beethoven's 9th symphony as groups of musical notes. They are much, much more than that. SI does not function in a vacuum but as a directly positive life force.

Visiting Japan, neurologist James Austin learned Zen meditation. It led him to compare it with his own training and experience. In a June 17, 2001 *Washington Post* interview he commented "I realized nothing in my training or experience prepared me for or helped me understand what was going on in my brain." Shakespeare's *Hamlet* put it well: "There are more things in heaven and earth than are dreamt of in our philosophy"

2. Evolutionary plausibility. Teilhard's *hominization to omega* satisfies this criterion. Charles Darwin observed in his *Origin of species* (1859): "In the distant future I see open fields for far more important research. Psychology will be based on a new foundation of the necessary acquirement of each mental power and capacity by gradation." Alfred North Whitehead wrote: "Religion persistently shows an upward trend. It fades then recurs and when it recurs it renews its force with an added richness and purity of content." And Walt Whitman observed: "There is no false religion. Each is divine and the state of development by-and-by will pass on farther" (*Notes for lectures*).

3. Identifiable core operations. Core operations of SI are the 16 S-traits described previously. They are evident in people and in the spiritual qualities reflected in the arts and humanities.

4. Personal and social meaning and values. Certainly, the history of religion and spiritual content of all the ancient moral codes meet this criterion. Before and after 9/11, Seligman and Peterson studied "character strengths" with 4817 Internet questionnaires that measured 24 traits on a 5-point scale. Seven "theological virtues" changed after

9/11: gratitude, hope/optimism, kindness, leadership, love/intimacy, spirituality, and teamwork. No other "secular character strengths" changed. They concluded the impact of 9/11 restored the need to share with others and grow spiritually.

5. *Distinct developmental history and end state.* Lawrence Kohlberg's 1984 model of moral development is the standard reference in psychology. It is described in Chapter 2 under the S-trait of moral maturity. It begins with "doing the right thing" and progresses through cooperating with others, respect for law and order, to the highest level, "universal ethical principles." Others have suggested a level or stage system. Fowler listed six stages "that shape relatedness to a transcendent center" in his book *Stages of faith* (1981). It begins with an "intuitive projective" stage and ends in a "universalizing" stage. Oser (1991) listed seven "moral dimensions" based on choices: freedom or dependence; transcendence or immanence; hope or absurdity; explanation or mystery; faith or fear; holy or profane; eternity or ephemerality.

6. *Gifted examples.* Clearly, Moses, Buddha, LaoTse, Jesus, and Muhammad are gifted examples of SI. There are many other examples of high-SI artists, composers, writers, and leaders. The many quotes throughout this book are also examples.

7. *Discrete experimental tasks, abilities, and skills.* Tasks, abilities, and skills of the founders, the leaders and followers of religions, personality theorists, artists, writers, and composers are replete with discrete tasks, abilities,

and skills. Research data such as brain studies described earlier in this book offer further evidence.

8. *Psychometric evidence that differs from traditional intelligence.* The *Spiritual Awareness Inventory* in Chapter 1 is one of several other self-tests and surveys. Hill and Hood (1999) reviewed 125 religiosity and spirituality measures. Dean Hoge developed the *Validated Intrinsic Religious Motivation Scale* based on Allport's concept of intrinsic and extrinsic religion. Hall and Edwards (2002) created the *Spiritual Assessment Inventory (SAI)* called "a theistic model and measure" of "psychospiritual development." These and other tests, surveys, and question- naires satisfy this criterion.

In addition to "Gardner's eight" criteria, there are two others that differentiate SI from other intelligences:

Distinctive behavior. Islamic extremists claim to be morally justified in killing "infidels." This is inconsistent with SI (or the *Qu'ran*). There are many instances in history of violence justified as moral. SI is non-violent, positive, and unifying. Anything violent, negative, or divisive is not SI.

Distinctive spiritual quality. In addition to the history of religion and related philosophies, the world's arts and humanities reflect a distinctive spiritual quality. Rodin's sculpture, Michelangelo's art, Shakespeare's writings, and Mozart's music are some of many more examples.

Psychology has resisted researching religion and spirituality. What little has been researched is a fraction of psychology's total database which studies only what can be observed, measured, and proved. If it fails that test it either doesn't exist or is not worthy of study. It's a numbers game of norms and curves, levels and stages. Individual differences are often lost. Excluding data is unscientific!

Psychology's resistance to SI is the result of a century of bias. In the 19th century psychology was the *study of the mind*. John Watson's attack on Freud and his narrow focus only on observed behavior changed the definition to *the study of behavior*. B. F. Skinner fought against adding *mental processes* to the definition. He lost. The current definition: *Psychology is the study of behavior and mental processes*. That it took until the 1960s to include mental processes clearly exposes psychology's bias.

Personality theories began with the knowledge and experience of their founders. They were careful observers who worked in good faith but were limited by their unique perception. Today they would likely be rejected as too subjective. That's a theoretical bias. On the plus side, early theorists were free to take intuitive leaps when "hard data" was not available. Some included references to religion in their work. Another red flag! Those who saw religion as positive to personality development were seminal thinkers. Among them are Allport, Fromm, Maslow, and Rogers, to name but a few. There are more.

Gordon Allport spent his career searching for a unified personality theory. He did not succeed but saw spiritual awareness as a necessary part of personality. He wrote that "a psychology that impedes understanding religious potentialities scarcely deserves to be called a logos of the human psyche at all" (1955). Claudio Naranjo saw value even in mystic thought: "Psychotherapy and esotericism are different stages in a single journey, a continuous process of consciousness expansion, integration, and self-realization."

Mainstream psychology may be awakening to the reality of mental processes such as SI. Mazharin Banaji, at the 2001 American Psychological Society, spoke of a "third revolution." She said the first revolution was when Galileo proved the earth rotated around the sun, heresy at the time. The second revolution started with Darwin's theory of evolution. She called the third revolution "the hardest of them all" because it's "about the very nature of our minds, about our goodness, our ability to be moral and to have control over our thoughts and feelings, about the most important object in our universe: other humans" (*APS Observer*, July-August 2001).

A hundred years ago, P. D. Ouspensky was a voice in the wilderness with a similar message. He traveled in Egypt, India, and Ceylon "to seek the miraculous." In his 1962 book *The psychology of man's possible evolution* he described a psychology open to the study of whatever the mind perceives. The book was published as American psychology debated whether to allow mental processes in its definition. Ouspensky wrote: "The psychology of which I speak is very different from anything you may know under that name." He saw its current state as a focus on "the artificial person without studying the real person."

MASLOW'S VISION

Abraham Maslow was a psychologist who began as a behaviorist and became a humanistic psychologist as he studied normal people. His career is an example of how the worlds of science and religion can merge to their mutual benefit. He felt the need to help people fully realize themselves and found that therapy alone does not meet that need: "There is a resurgence of more sophisticated forms of the old identification of psychological health with adjustment, the usual goal of therapy" (1968).

Maslow agreed adjustment is important but "we must leap beyond to a clear recognition of transcendence." In his words: "Adequacy, adjustment, adaptation, mastery, competence, and coping do not describe the whole psyche, part of which has nothing to do with the environment. It's in a different context and involves a different mental process because expressive behavior is not directed at coping or changing the environment."

Self-actualization is the highest level in Maslow's needs list. He found self-actualizers show "signs of becoming" he called B-values and "show interest outside one's own psyche." Art, literature, music, or history "come alive" to them and they "rise above culture like a tree with roots in the soil but branches high above" and "examine their culture in a detached and objective way" in "a Taoist attitude "of harmony with nature and with their natures.

They "accept the world as it is" but see the ideal, what could be, with "a mystical quality like Thy will be done." He explained his choice of the word mystical: "I mean here the experience described by religious mystics in religious literature that transcends death, pain, and illness." Is self-actualization and SI the same? No. Results of the *Spiritual Awareness Inventory* and interviews with high scorers suggest they are similar but not identical. Here are the B-values and the S-traits:

B-VALUES

1. Truth	8. Completion
2. Goodness	9. Justice
3. Beauty	10. Simplicity
4. Unity, wholeness	11. Richness
5. Aliveness	12. Effortlessness
6. Uniqueness	13. Playfulness
7. Necessity	14. Self-sufficiency

15. Meaningfulness

SI S-TRAITS

1. Meditative awareness
2. Esthetic awareness
3. Moral maturity
4. Character, integrity
5. Empathy
6. Openness
7. Growth drive
8. Selfless service
9. Modesty, humility
10. Compassion, caring
11. Positive attitude
12. Elegant simplicity
13. Spontaneity
14. Honest candor
15. Spiritual introjection
16. Spiritual humor

PEAK EXPERIENCES

Self-actualizers have *peak* or *oceanic experiences* which Maslow (1970) described as "experiences that can equally be called religious experiences, poetic experiences, or also philosophical experiences. They are moments of wonder, awe, and insight. They often occur in serene detachment "getting so absorbed in something one forgets where one is." They can be triggered by a beautiful sunrise or sunset, moving music, reading, even in conversation. Afterward there is a feeling of "illumination and insight." There is "a spectator-like objectivity in which one cannot unsee, be naïve, innocent, or ignorant again in the same way." There is a spiritual quality in a "rise to the very highest sense in which one is identified with the whole human species." High SI is conducive to peak experiences and likely to have a spiritual quality.

EXERCISE 13. *Have you had an oceanic or peak experience? How would you know it if you have one? Try to be receptive to them and ready to fully experience them.*

TRANSCENDERS

Maslow (1968) found another trait, *transcending*. He called those who have it *transcenders*. He explained his choice of the word: "*Transcending* is to do more than one thought one could do, to become divine or godlike, go beyond the merely human but not extrahuman or super-natural." Maslow found they had "a higher transcendent nature that is part of our essence and a potentiality of human nature" and they "easily, normally, naturally, and unconsciously speak the language of Being, the language of poets, mystics, seers and the profoundly religious."

Transcenders also "have a way of going into self." This inner self has a childlike quality of openness, a kind of "divine daydreaming, prior to good or evil." Writers have referred to it as the Eternal Child in everyone. Erich Fromm (1951) called it "the source of creativity, art, love, humor, and play with a dynamic force of its own." For Eric Berne it was the *natural child* or *OK Kid,* one of three parts of the personality (Harris, 1969). This trait is also suggested in pictures of infant angels.

Transcenders see "the sacred within the secular" in parables, music, art, and literature. Maslow described them as able to become "more ecstatic, more rapturous" than others. They have "an intrinsic conscience and are godlike, more saintly in the medieval sense." They "seem somehow to recognize each other and come to almost instant intimacy and mutual understanding."

The child in us fades with age. R. D. Laing (1972) wrote: "To adapt to this world the child abdicates its ecstasy." Maslow, too, saw this gradual weakening but thought it was still within reach "like the voice of the intellect, it speaks softly but can be heard." Ignoring it, he warned, can cause "justified self-disapproval because it is a betrayal of one's own inner nature or self, turning off the path to self-actualization."

There is a down side. Maslow found "a kind of cosmic sadness or B-sadness over stupidity, self-defeat, or cruelty in themselves, others, and the world due to directly seeing the saintly possibilities in human nature." He estimated there are as many transcenders in business, government, and industry as in "the professionally religious, poets, intellectuals, musicians, and others who are *supposed* to be transcenders." He found some clergy "who talk transcendence but haven't the slightest inkling of what it feels like." Maslow estimated there are many transcenders outside organized religion and are often self-conscious and conceal their experiences from others.

EXERCISE 14. *Are you a transcender? Have you met any? How can you improve your openness to a transcending experience?*

THEORY Z

Maslow found that not all self-actualizers are transcenders, and vice versa. He found two types of self-actualizer: those who are transcenders, and those who are not. He reported that "all transcenders are meta-motivated. Peak experiences change them, their world view, and become the most precious aspects of life. They speak the B-language of artists and poets, writers and composers, mystics and the deeply spiritual" and have "a natural tendency to synergy, intrapsychic, interpersonal, interculturally and internationally." They are "innovators, discoverers" with a "natural aura of greatness, less happy in the traditional sense since they crave what most people are not even aware of."

There is a parallel in SI to Maslow's two self-actualizer types: *SI literals* and *mystics*. *Literals* follow orderly guidelines and a code of moral conduct usually based on scripture. *Mystics* are in the minority since they tend to be loners in their search for truth. They are most like Maslow's *transcenders*. They "read between the lines" and search beyond guidelines and scripture. *Literals* read. *Mystics* reflect. This may be how Socrates, Buddha, LaoTse, Moses, Jesus, and Muhammad differed from others.

There is a difference between how science defines what life is and an SI awareness of what life means. Science needs to *prove*, religion needs to *profess*, and SI seeks to *transcend*. All share a search for truth but from different directions. A 4th view would be to accept all three of them as aspects of the same search. Buddha did much the same using a diamond as an example, each facet true but only an aspect of whole truth. That view is consistent with high level SI.

While visiting Japan, neurologist James Austin studied Zen meditation. It led him to reflect on his own training and experience. In a *Washington Post* interview June 17, 2001, he said: "I realized that nothing in my training or experience prepared me for or helped me understand what was going on in my brain." Shakespeare put it well in *Hamlet*: "There are more things in heaven and earth than are dreamt of in our philosophy."

EXERCISE 15. *Can you see how psychology and religion differ in how they seek truth? Can you see how they can complement each other? SI is psychological because it is a genetic personality trait but it is also religious because of its spiritual distinctive spiritual quality.*

Psychiatry has been more open to studying mental processes similar to SI. In his 1930 book *The human mind*, Karl Menninger, one of psychiatry's grand old men, wrote: "Mental health includes all the healths -- physical, social, cultural, and moral-spiritual. To live, to love, to care, to enjoy, to build on the foundations of our predecessors, to revere the constant miracles of creation, the starry skies above and moral law within, these are acts and attitudes that express mental health."

Freud (1933) saw religion as "an illusion that derives its strength from instinctual desires." Though it may seem negative, it is consistent with Teilhard's concept of an *evolving spirituality* linking instinct and religion in the process of *hominization* to *omega*. Freud might well have been receptive to it. Freud and Teilhard were not that far apart. Freud was a skeptic but his mind was not closed. He conceded that "the characteristic features of childish helplessness lend themselves to the formation of religion" (1927). There is a more positive reference is in his 1933 *New introductory lectures on psychoanalysis*: "To form a true estimate of the full grandeur of religion, one must keep in mind what it undertakes to do. It gives information about the source and origin of the universe, assures protection and final happiness amid the changing vicissitudes of life, and guides thoughts and emotions by precepts backed by the force of authority."

Carl Jung had a similar view. In *The secret of the golden flower* he wrote: "All religions are therapies for the sorrows and disorders of the soul." Charles Francis Potter, in his book *Great religious leaders*, wrote: "Religion is the endeavor of divided and incomplete human personality to attain unity and completion." That process blends the spiritual and psychological. They are coexist, are interactive and necessary for mental health and also spiritual growth.

There is evidence in the mental health field of a slow awakening to SI and its value. There is a trend in therapy to add a "non-denominational spirituality" and personal value system to treatment goals. Most treatment plans end with "improved coping skills," when a person is "well adjusted," or a disorder is "in remission." Little attention is given to developing spiritual awareness or a personal value system.

Alcoholics Anonymous uses a non-denominational spirituality in its program. One of their 12 steps refers to "a higher power" outside of one's self for recovery. Many scientists have looked outside their selves in the search for truth. Albert Einstein wrote that "the cosmic religious experience is the strongest, noblest driving force behind scientific research." Carl Sagan agreed: "Science is not only compatible with spirituality, it is a profound source of spirituality." There is what has been called the researcher's credo: "An experiment is a question put to God" (anonymous).

EXERCISE 16. *Can you see how psychology, psychiatry, and religion are on parallel yet separate courses in their search for truth? Can you see how collaboration would be to their mutual benefit?*

SI SPARKS

41. The most beautiful thing we can experience is the mysterious. It is the source of all true art and science (Albert Einstein).
42. Science is a first-rate piece of furniture for the upper chamber if you have common sense on the ground floor (Oliver Wendell Holmes).
43. I cannot say I believe. I know. I have had the experience of being gripped by something bigger than myself, something people call God (Carl Jung, *Time* magazine, February 14, 1955).
44. A little learning is a dangerous thing. Drink deep or taste not the Pierian spring (Alexander Pope).

45. It is the way of scholars to show all they know and oppose further information (Francis Bacon, in the *Advancement of learning*, 1805).

46. Learn your theories well but put them aside when you confront the mystery of the soul (Carl Jung).

47. To study any subject scientifically one needs a detached attitude, obviously harder when one's own interests or emotions are involved (George Orwell).

47. I have great faith in science, real science, of the soul as well as the body. Many men of half science forget the soul (Walt Whitman).

48. People have to awaken to wonder. Science is a way of putting them to sleep again (Ludwig Wittgenstein).

49. Scientism is authority set above free inquiry (Philip Wylie, in *Generation of vipers*, 1942).

50. Lying plays an important part in life. We cannot know all the truth but we pretend we know. People pretend they know about God, the universe, evolution, every thing but in reality they don't know, even about them selves (P. D. Ouspensky, in *The psychology of man's possible evolution*, 1962).

6

SI IN THE ARTS AND HUMANITIES

> Beauty is truth, truth beauty.
> That is all you know and all
> you need to know
> -- John Keats
> *Ode on a Grecian Urn*

Because SI expands consciousness it is related to the arts and humanities. Whatever is spiritually moving in art, music, and literature is an SI S-trait. That makes the arts and humanities rich sources of data to validate SI. It identifies useful ways to help develop SI. Being moved by art, music, or reading is a freeing experience. The consciousness expands, even if for a moment. Those are the divine sparks of high SI. They have inspired artists, composers, and writers and energize those who later experience their works.

Paul Camus described this freeing effect in *Resistance, rebellion, and death* (1957): "There is not a single true work of art that has not in the end added to the inner freedom of each person who has known and loved it." This from a leader of the "God is dead" French existentialists! Many were anti-religious yet spiritual! It is part of human nature to reach up and out to something higher, greater. In *Courage to be happy* (1957), Dorothy Thompson wrote "the liberation of great art is to lift us out of ourselves." Alfred North Whitehead wrote about art's spiritual dimension in his book *Science and the modern world* (1925): "Art adds to the permanent richness of the soul's self-attainment and transforms the soul into the permanent realization of values extending beyond its former self." In *Conduct of life*, Lewis Mumford summed it up as "the timelessness of art is its capacity to represent the transformation of endless becoming into being,"

The works of authors and artists who optimized their SI reflect a spiritual quality. Divine sparks fly! Since SI is in everyone, experiencing great works connects with that divine spark and the higher power behind it. That spark is available to anyone who is receptive to it. Ralph Waldo Emerson observed: "All high beauty has a moral element in it." And John Keats: "A thing of beauty is a joy forever" (*Endymion*, 1818). Here is an overview of SI in the arts and humanities:

AESTHETICS is a branch of philosophy that studies what is considered beauty in art and nature. The so-called *Seven Wonders of the World* were material objects that were beautiful in their appearance and the effect on those who saw them. They were built as much for those living at the time as for posterity. Plato talked of *archetypes of forms*, the perfect or ideal humans can strive to create but never fully achieve. Aristotle described art as "partly completing what nature cannot finish." Plotinus saw art as raising consciousness to a higher level he called *The One*.

In 1750, Baumgarten used the term aesthetics to describe a "science of sensuous knowledge" that is more inductive than deductive and not based only on logic or reason. Immanuel Kant continued this idea with the term *transcendental aesthetic*. He explained anything of beauty is transcending, whether seen as such or not. Schopenhauer felt deepest personal satisfaction from experiencing beauty for its own sake. Hegel saw art, philosophy, and religion as paths to higher spiritual awareness.

Avant-garde impressionism entered 19th century art, music, and literature. Cezanne, Gauguin, Matisse, Monet, Picasso, Van Gogh and others painted their perception of beauty and became known as impressionists. Berlioz, Debussy, Ravel, Prokofiev, Satie, and others did the same in music. This movement continued with Frank Lloyd Wright in architecture, Beckett and Brecht in drama, Stanislavski in acting, Camus and Sartre in existentialism. All are examples of ways to perceive beauty from nature and by one's own nature and create something elegant.

Maslow wrote: "Esthetic perception and peak experiences are a central aspect of human life. Science and education do not have a place for esthetic experience, especially the subjective happenings inside one's self" (1968). Esthetic awareness is an important aspect of SI and an S-trait.

ALCHEMY is the ancient science that sought to transform (*transmute*) common into precious metals, such as lead to gold. It was believed precious metals were made from baser metals, so it should be possible to duplicate this process. Alchemy also sought to transform human nature into the divine. The basic idea is to create something from nothing, or life from the lifeless. That was the theme in Mary Wollstonecraft Shelley's *Frankenstein*. Its continuing popularity in print and visual media suggests it strikes a responsive chord.

In the Middle Ages, Albertus Magus in Germany and Roger Bacon in England kept alchemy alive. They believed there was a *philosopher's stone* more precious than gold and could be blended with common substances into a more perfect form. Today that idea inspires fine wines, gourmet foods, and metal alloys from more common materials. Therapy refines personality from its baser elements. Carl Jung saw alchemy as "inspired by the hope of solving one of the mysteries of life, the connection between good and evil, how the base aspects of life are transmuted into the noble" (Bennet, 1966).

Chinese alchemy was based on *the union of opposites* shown graphically the *Yin-Yang symbol*. Carl Jung used it to explain his concept of *anima* (feminine, *mystic mother*) and *animus* (masculine, *mystic father*), co-existing traits in men and women. He applied it in his concept of opposing traits such as extroversion and introversion, thinking and feeling, and sensing and intuiting.

ART. French sculptor Auguste Rodin considered art a form of contemplation: "Art is the pleasure of the mind searching nature and divining the spirit that animates it and the joy of intellect that clearly sees and recreates the universe." He saw artists as celebrating their souls and "enriching the soul of humanity, their most sublime mission." The test of spirituality of an art object, whether a photograph, painting, sculpture, or in architecture, is its "spiritual push" to remove the viewer from present thought, feeling, and even time and move upward to higher meditative awareness.

The difference between simple satisfaction and transcendence is a measure of SI level. Bernin's statue *Ecstasy of Teresa Avila* is in white marble, with solid bronze rays of light from above. Teresa reclines on a cloud as a winged angel aims an arrow at her heart. It can be seen as a fine piece of baroque art, which it is. Teresa of Avila was one of the world's great mystics. She described her "ecstasy" which she achieved by meditating but with chest pain she called "an arrow from God." The statue is a three-dimensional symbol of SI as a ray of light from above.

ARCHAEOLOGY literally unearths evidence to confirm history and the lives of people in historic times. Biblical archaeology focuses on the history of religion. Centuries ago archaeologists were faith-based, seeking evidence to validate "Bible truth." Over time, a more skeptical group emerged, called *minimalists*. They took no side, but considered alternatives. More recently *revisionists* have merged, denying anything not clearly proven. They represent an evolving philosophy that is more data-driven than faith-based. Some question whether Moses or Jesus really lived. These movements help in the search for truth by ensuring no data is omitted or theory overlooked.

Censoring the work of Copernicus and Galileo shows how literal belief can obstruct scientific progress. The sword of truth cuts both ways. Religion resists scientific research and science resists religion. An exception and model for future collaboration is the *Dead Sea Scrolls.* Jewish, Christian, and Muslim scholars collaborated. And modern imaging instruments deciphered and dated scroll fragments. Science and religion both got data they would not have had without their interaction.

ARCHITECTURE. The uplifting effect of the world's great architecture has a spiritual quality. We say it is "awe inspiring" or "awesome," whether it be the Taj Mahal or Eiffel Tower, the Great Pyramid of Egypt or Notre Dame Cathedral. Germany's great philosopher Wolfgang Goethe called architecture "petrified music." British architect

Christopher Wren described it as "aimed at eternity" and America's Frank Lloyd Wright saw it as "the great mother art behind which all the others are related." Winston Churchill wrote: "We shape our buildings, thereafter they shape us." The legendary seven wonders of the world were wonders because of their elegant beauty. They overwhelmed the senses, literally took your breath way. There is a spiritual quality in them. There is SI in architecture when it does more than "look good." This "spiritual high" can occur when experiencing a mountain, waterfall, or ocean beach — nature's architecture.

BIOGRAPHY AND HISTORY are rich sources of information on people and their personalities. Many showed high levels of SI. Lincoln is one example. Unlike current presidents he was the sole author of what he wrote and spoke. There is a distinct spiritual quality in his words. Carl Sandburg's biography has many examples. Commenting on armies of the north and south at war, Lincoln remarked: "Both read the same Bible and pray to the same God and each army invokes his aid against the other" ... "a house divided against itself cannot stand." He used many religious references such as "in the name of the Common Father ... God of Nations ... guiding Supreme Power."

A century before Teilhard, Lincoln saw how frailty and faith interact: "I believe God will let us go our own way to our ruin, but if we do right I believe he will lead us safely out of this wilderness." In his 1861 inaugural address he said: "We are not enemies but friends. We must not be enemies. Though passion may have strained, it must not break our bonds of affection. The mystic cords of memory stretching from every battlefield and patriot grave to every living heart and hearthstone all over this broad land will yet swell the chorus of the Union when again touched as surely they will be by the better angels of our nature."

Lincoln's SI was reflected in his behavior, especially when taken by surprise. In April 1865 he was walking in Richmond as it still burned. He was surrounded by a group of freed slaves. One knelt to kiss his hand. With both hands Lincoln lifted him gently and with calm reassurance said: "Do not kneel to me. You are free. Kneel only to God." His *Gettysburg Address* was as much spiritual as political. Though as far as is known he had no religious affiliation, we know he did read the Bible and often quoted from it. Sandburg described his spirituality: "A current of mysticism in Lincoln seemed to run parallel with a strain of rationalism. He was a sober and sad man whose lapses into wit or humor faded often into the austere or the abstract, a process of crystallization from interplay of the outside world and his own personality."

Biography is a rich source of data on the nature and qualities of SI. This is true of Erik Erikson's biographies of Gandhi and Luther. They describe their personalities and lives with insight into their works. Similar psychological explorations of spiritual leaders can provide information from that can help further define SI. The life and work of John Calvin (1509-1564 CE), founder of Presbyterianism, show how religion and SI are complementary. His views of universal brotherhood and grace are consistent with both religion and SI. In a letter to Cardinal Sadoleto in 1539, Calvin referred to doctrine, discipline, sacraments, and ceremonies as external signs of what should be an internal process of faith and spiritual growth.

EXISTENTIALISM. As we've seen, Howard Gardner, champion of multiple intelligences, no longer accepts a spiritual intelligence. In a 2000 journal article he wrote he considered SI an aspect of an existentialist intelligence. What a strange connection! Existentialism is related to phenomenology and Zen Buddhism not simply defined and with many variations, but it is also closely related to the militant atheism of Friedrich Nietzsche, Jean Paul Sartre's agnosticism, and the transcendent consciousness of Karl Jaspers. But there is a common element: relying on individual freedom and responsibility. Sartre's seemingly simple 2-part admonition is typical of this approach: "You are free. Define yourself!" Existentialists see limitations to knowledge and that absolute truth is largely unknowable. Truth can seem as much abstract as concrete, subjective as much as objective.

What makes spiritual sense may not make logical sense, evidenced in the questioning of Socrates, Plato's reflections, Aristotle's "need to know," and Pascal's paradoxes. Nietzsche claimed the important aspects of life were beyond the reach of science and reason. He called scientific explanations "useful fiction. Soren Kierkegaard is considered the father of existentialism. He described the quality of life as one of "dread," caused by ambiguity and uncertainty. He saw this as God's way to motivate us to find ourselves. That opens the door to a more positive view. Sartre claimed "existence precedes essence." Jaspers said "existence rests on transcendence."

Existentialists are skeptical about rigid interpretations and fixed systems because of their firm stand on personal freedom. As a result there is little agreement among them.

If there was agreement their approach would become fixed, no longer open to a free search. They are criticized as anti-intellectual, unscientific, or selfish. But the statement "there is no meaning to life" challenges us to find meaning. That's similar to the goal of religion, though it may seem anti-religious. SI is compatible with this aspect of existentialism because it is a personal process not bound by religion.

There have been existentialist thinkers in organized religion such as Gabriel Marcel (Roman Catholic), Nikolai Berdyayev (Russian Orthodox), Paul Tillich (Protestant), and Martin Buber (Jewish). In literature, existentialist ideas are in the works of Fyodor Dostoevsky, Franz Kafka, John Updike, Norman Mailer, John Barth, and Arthur Miller.

POETRY. William Wordsworth considered poetry "the spontaneous overflow of powerful feelings, its origin in emotion, and recollected in tranquility." His description of a poet's function: "In spite of different soil and climate, language and manners, laws and customs, in spite of things silently gone out of mind and things violently destroyed, the poet binds together the vast empire of human society as it is spread over the whole earth and over time" (Beck, 1968).

When he was 13, John Masefield ran away from home. He spent six years at sea. During those formative years there was much time for reflection. Years later he wrote of the sea and the meaning of life. His writing earned him the title of Poet Laureate. He thought "we create living mental images according to our strength" and poets put "intense life" into their writing. Poets "touch energy, the source of everything, the reality behind all appearance." They "are made one with nature, their work perfected by the force of life itself." To Percy Bysshe Shelley poetry was "the very image of life expressed in its eternal truth, an interpenetration of a divine nature through our own, all that is best and most beautiful, immortal because it redeems us from decay by visitations of divinity."

DRAMA. Sophocles and Shakespeare are two of many playwrights with a deep understanding of human nature and word craft to portray it. Freud referred to them often and Ibsen's plays were among his favorites. The Oedipus complex is evidence of the influence of Sophocles' plays. Part of Shakespeare's genius was his awareness of mental processes. *Othello, MacBeth, and Hamlet* were stories of the force of normal emotions gone to extremes. Modern drama explores the best and worst of human nature. Examples: *Les miserables, Streetcar named Desire, Death of a salesman, a*nd *The crucible.*

PROSE is another rich source of examples of SI. John Ruskin said there are two kinds of books, "books of the hour" and "books for all time." Books of the hour are by "authors with something to say, what to them is true, useful, or beautiful." Books for all time are written "in all ages by their greatest men (sic)." They are "electric forces" and make "an ennobling difference" from books of the time. Prose that endures make readers think and feel what the book's characters think and feel. This has been true from Homer through Chaucer to Dickens to Hemingway, and today's best sellers. SI-rich books have a long shelf life and live longer in the minds of readers. They are often quoted from one generation to another. There are examples quoted throughout this book.

METAPHYSICS is a branch of philosophy, the study of the nature of ultimate reality and what transcends it. Its western roots date back to Greek philosopher Andronicus of Rhodes (c. 100 BCE). It is said he called Aristotle's *First Philosophy* and *Physics* to be *meta* physics, beyond physics. Metaphysics attempts to define what is real and true throughout the universe and across all time. It was only a matter of time before it clashed with religion which was more structured and closed. They had similar goals in the search for the meaning of life.

Religion prefers fixed, simple definitions and a clear distinction between what is right and wrong. That's the message in *Genesis* when God forbade Adam and Eve to partake of the forbidden fruit. That fruit was on the tree of knowledge. Metaphysics not only eats that fruit but wonders if there are other trees and different fruits. It can have no limits to its search for truth and ultimate reality. There is a danger in extremes from too little or too much freedom and this has happened to both religion and metaphysics.

Before Immanual Kant, research was by reason alone without experiential knowledge. Kant synthesized several concepts into what he called *transcendental metaphysics* or *transcendentalism*. Just because there is little or no research data to support a hypothesis does not mean it is not valid. Kant recommended that experience should be substituted for research data. He wrote: "It should be interpreted holistically to realize even higher truth." He predicted a synergistic effect, that when factors interact they would exceed their sum. That's the Zen "mystic leap" and the process that leads to discoveries beyond known facts. It is intuitive awareness consistent with high SI.

Like Leibnitz, Kant believed the mind contains ideas not yet clearly understood. This is similar to Freud's unconscious mind, as if we are mentally hard-wired ready to discover what is in the mind and use it to help search for what is not yet here -- Teilhard's *hominization* to *omega*. Clearing and freeing the mind prepares the way to expand consciousness. It is an aspect of SI, moving onward from known to unknown, from what is to what can be, from mundane to meaningful to the magnificent.

MUSIC is a universal language. Composers speak to us in this elegant language across time, language, and culture. Plato said "music gives a soul to the universe." Beethoven said: "What I have in my heart and soul must find a way out. That is the reason for music." Dance, music, and opera reflect the SI of the composer and when they are especially moving experiences, in the performers.

Orchestral music combines instruments, musicians, composer, conductor, and score. In a kind of mystic moment, when all the parts mesh together, they emit a divine spark. That energy is often reflected in a critic's description of a performance. High SI music can be soft or slow such as Barber's *Adagio for Strings*, Beethoven's *Moonlight Sonata*, Debussy's *Claire de lune*, Lizst's *Liebestraum*, Pachelbel's *Canon*, or Ravel's *Pavane for a dead princess*.

Musical language is expressed in many ways. It can be in the rhythmic melodies of Mozart or the powerful spiritual push of Bach's B-minor mass, Beethoven's 9th choral symphony, Saint-Saen's 3rd organ symphony, or Richard Strauss' *Ein Heldenleben*. Rachmaninoff's 3rd piano concerto has been described as having a "mystic quality." Music can express deep emotion as the depth and power of love in the adagio movement in Khatchaturian's *Spartacus* and Tchaikovsky's *Romeo and Juliet*. The opening bars of Prokofiev's version of *Romeo and Juliet* are a musical scream of outrage at the unfolding tragedy.

Song. Spirituals and hymns are ways of sharing spiritual consciousness. *Ave Maria* and *Amazing Grace* are examples. This sharing can occur in opera, musicals, and popular songs. The *Flower song* duet in Leo Delibes' *Lackme* sparkles with esthetic elegance. The physical setting can add to the magic of music. One cannot help but be moved sitting in the Cathedral of Notre Dame. The floor vibrates from the powerful organ – and so does the listener's spirit. There is a spiritual uplift listening to child and adult carolers singing *Silent Night* on a winter night. SI can be stimulated by *Panis Angelicus, Ave Verum*, Andrew Lloyd Webber's *Pia Jesu, The Shaker Hymn* (Copland), *Danny Boy, Greensleave*, or orchestra and chorus performing Handel's *Messiah*.

Musicals and opera blend drama, dance, and music, with visual effects. Machlos called opera "drama that is sung" (1963). Often, everyday people are portrayed in stressful situations that end well or in tragedy. Opera is much like the morality plays of ancient Greece. It becomes an SI stimulant when music, song, and audience share the same musical message it becomes an SI exercise. In a CBS TV interview, Richard Rodgers' daughter said of her father: "Music was as close to God as he would ever get." Songs like *You'll never walk alone* in *Carousel* and *Somewhere* in *West Side Story* bring tears to many. Music and song in *Show Boat, Oklahoma. Les Miserables, Evita, Cats*, and *Phantom of the Opera* have had similar effect.

Richard Wagner wrote both words and music in his operas. About the love duet and love death in *Liebestod* he said: "Life and death, the whole significance of existence of the external world, turn on nothing but the inner movements of the soul." He explored mystical thought in *Flying Dutchman* and *Ring of the Nibelung*. Jacques Offenbach did, too, in *Tales of Hoffmann*. Giuseppe Verdi's *Aida* is set in ancient Egypt and musically describes mystic chants, rituals, dances, and songs of love (*Celeste Aida*). Life, love, and death are common themes in Puccini's *La Boheme* and *Madame Butterfly*, Bizet's *Carmen*, Gounod's *Faust*, and Delibes' *Lakme*. Humperdinck set the innocence of childhood to music in *Hansel and Gretel*. *The children's prayer* radiates high SI.

Opera has been popular for centuries, enjoyed by people who differ in age, language, and culture. The test of time is evidence they satisfy a shared need. In them, cast, orchestra, and audience are swept together toward tragedy or transcendence. Done well, they trigger not only an emotional response but compassion, inspiration, and transcendence, features of SI.

Dance has been called "the body singing." Like music, dance is a universal language with high SI potential. From earliest times dance has been part of rituals and ceremonies. Dance has been used to celebrate events and to express feelings of the moment. Musical background sets the psychological stage and together, music and dance can uplift the spirit. In Native American dance, women move in short measured steps as men dance forcefully. The theme is often one of reverence for nature. Chanting together dancers, drummers, and audience become prayers in motion. In folk dance, there are often smiles of joy as music, song, and dance blend. In classical ballet moving music, colorful costumes, and skilled dancers combine in what can be a transcending experience for performers and audience.

MYSTICISM has been a part of religion but never a popular movement of and by itself. It is therefore not possible to trace it to a single person. There is mystic thought in the Hindu Vedas, the world's most ancient known scripture. The content was chanted long before there was writing. That dates them to more than 5000 years. The Upanishads in the Vedas describe a higher reality than the external world. It is a mystic unity or ultimate real self, realized in awareness beyond everyday reality.

Mysticism is difficult to define because it is based on personal experience and intuitive awareness. Mystics search for deeper meanings in natural, paranormal, or supernatural events that connect to a higher consciousness. The word was first used by Dionysius Areopagite (ca. 500 CE). The Hindu and Buddhist interpretation of reality is it is more illusion and can even be delusional. That is a mystic concept. We do tend to see what we want to see. In *The Tempest*, one of Shakespeare's last plays:
"We are such stuff as dreams are made on and our life is rounded with a sleep." Edgar Allan Poe penned a similar thought: "All that we see or seem is but a dream within a dream."

The Taoist poet ChuangTse (369-286 BCE) wrote he dreamt he was a butterfly. He reflected: "I do not know if I was a man dreaming of being a butterfly or I am now a butterfly dreaming I am a man." Russian mystic Georgi

Gurdjieff described the mental state of most people as like being asleep. Buddha used the same metaphor.

Mystic awareness is a personal experience but it has been enhanced in groups such as the Mystery cults of ancient Rome, Greece, and Egypt. Three cults competed with early Christianity: Mithraism in the Roman legions; Cult of Asklepios in Greece where Hippocrates was a priest-physician; and the Cult of Isis-Osiris in Egypt. There are few mystical ideas in major religions. The highest level of consciousness in Hinduism is *Brahman*, achieved through *moksha* "mystic liberation."

Buddha's "middle way" or "message from the heart" leads to enlightenment (*Nibbana* or *Nirvana*). It is the *Tao* of LaoTse, achieved by *Teh*, virtue or character. It is in Zen *satori* flashes of insight. There is mystic thought among the Sufis of Islam and Hassidic and Kabbalist Jews, and in the writings of Christian mystics such as Augustine, John of the Cross, John the Baptist, John the Evangelist, Francis of Assisi, and Teresa of Avila, and many of the martyrs. Thomas Merton described mystic experience in *Faith and violence* (1968):

> Contemplative wisdom is not simply an
> esthetic extrapolation of certain intellectual
> or dogmatic principles, but a living contact
> with the Infinite Source of all being, not only
> of mind and heart or "I and Thou" but a
> transcendent union of consciousness in
> which God and man become "one spirit."

Sufism, a mystic component of Islam, began in the Middle Ages. There were mystics in the Middle East long before Muhammad, though use of the word *Sufi* dates only to the 19th century. They were known as "near ones, masters, people of truth." Like mystic thinkers of other religions, Sufis see all spiritual thought as an intuitive perception. They also see the human race as asleep but able to awaken to free itself and move upward to a higher consciousness. Like Zen use of koans, they often assign stories to open followers to mystic awareness.

MYTH AND LEGEND. Joseph Campbell was a prolific writer and authority on myths and their meaning. His books are worth reading and re-reading. He wrote: "Mythic figures are to be understood as embodiments and custodians of the Elixir of Imperishable Being" (1976). Campbell considered myths truths told in stories and symbols long before writing. They were often about creation or stories of heroic persons or deities. Carl Jung agreed: "Myths existed long before science and express life as it is seen and experienced more accurately than is objective scientific assessment" (Bennet, 1966). Thomas Merton described myth as "an imaginative synthesis of facts and intuitions forming an interpretive complex of ideas and images" (1968). Myths explain what is not yet fully   understood and they preserve ancient rituals and traditions.

Legends are stories of special events or situations in the lives of heroic figures. There is the legend of Davy Crockett who "kilt himself a bear when he was only three." Doubtful. Another is the little Dutch boy who saved his village by plugging a leak in a dike with his thumb. It would be possible if others arrived in time to help. Legends can be true, false, or mixed fact and fiction. Freud saw myth and legend beginning as unconscious wish fulfillment. To Jung, they reflected archetypal imagery within the whole human race. Myth and legend are methods of insight learning when they describe admirable behavior and ideals to emulate.

THE OCCULT (L."to hide"), or occultism, is the study of sources of hidden meaning or esoteric wisdom. Often, what is not clearly understood leads to an occult explanation. In ancient times such events and ideas were usually seen as the will or whim of gods. Those who were mentally ill in medieval Europe were believed to be possessed by a devil. Astrology was a way to understand personality dynamics before psychology offered more valid methods. At the time the occult was called "the black arts" or "work of the devil" and led to torture and execution for witchcraft. There was renewed interest in the occult in the Renaissance and by the 18th and 19th centuries study of the occult was seen as a way to seek spiritual meaning.

Colin Wilson's book *The Occult, a History* (1971) is an excellent reference on the subject. Wilson describes occult study as like trying to see a beautiful panorama through slats of a high fence. He sees consciousness as being as limited as that, lulling us into "a state of permanent drowsiness." This is the "sleep" Gurdjieff used to describe the mental state of most people. Wilson adds that it narrows vision. It can be "as powerful as a microscope to grasp and analyze experience." He suggests we develop "another kind of consciousness equivalent to a telescope." He calls that "faculty X" and comments: "The paradox is we already possess to a large degree but are unconscious of possessing it. It lies at the heart of all so-called occult experience."

PHENOMENOLOGY is an aspect of SI difficult to define. It is the study of perception and experience without objective or subjective interpretation. It studies what is, as is and that makes it similar to Zen. Others define it as the science of the subjective or the study of unique individual perception. David Hume saw mental percepts as the only pure knowledge. To him knowledge *is* experience.

Hegel referred to individual interpretation as "the phenomenology of mind." Husserl is considered the father of phenomenology as a system of philosophy. He defined it as "what shows itself." That includes one's own thought processes and whatever transcends them. There is intent because mental processes have direction -- they point somewhere – and that endows them with meaning and purpose. Husserl was a forerunner of what he called "an eidetic science of transcendental subjectivity" that is "intersubjectively valid" and is "a transcendental-phenomenological idealism" (Runes, 1976).

A phenomenological approach is the open, unbiased attitude of an uninvolved spectator. It is similar to the "naturalistic observation" research method of science. One is aware of what is happening without taking any part in it actively or passively to change it. In his hypnosis research Ernest Hilgard described a similar state of mind in hypnosis. He called it *the hidden observer*. A hypnotized person is aware of what is happening but it is as if outside one's body. It is the research ideal of "letting the data take you where it will." A step along Buddha's 8-fold path is *mindfulness*. It is an S-trait and demonstrates how science and religion again come face to face.

SYMBOLS portray concepts in graphic form and prove the adage: "A picture is worth a thousand words." Symbols preceded language and are the oldest form of communication. Examples are inscriptions on cave walls and petroglyphs on rocks of animals, people, sun, moon, mountains and rivers. Power was visualized as mountains, oceans, rivers and floods. Life was depicted by animals, people, birds, fish, and trees. Freud and Jung used this thinking in interpreting dreams.

The Star of David and cross, the current symbols of Judaism and Christianity, are much older. The cross was used in pre-Columbian America and ancient Asia. They showed the interaction of earth, the horizontal line, and human life or higher consciousness, the vertical line. The two superimposed triangles of the Star of David appear also in Islamic mausoleums of Arabic Sultans. Like the cross, it symbolizes earthbound life in the triangle pointing down, and higher aspirations or consciousness in the triangle pointing upward. The bases of both triangles are on the level plane suggesting earthly and spiritual life is related and within reach of each other, separate but equal.

There are many ancient symbols of the interaction of two equal forces. Examples are the yin-yang symbol of Taoism, 2-headed eagle of ancient Rome, and two snakes intertwined in pre-Columbian America and ancient Greece, Rome, and Persia. The swastika, also called a twisted cross, was used centuries before Hitler's Nazism on tepees of Native Americans. It is currently the symbol of China's Falun Gong. The ancients found meaning in its rotation, absorbing or radiating energy depending on the direction of movement. The yin-yang symbol can be used the same way to show sudden or gradual change.

COLOR has been used throughout history to symbolize emotional tone. In national flags blue is used to symbolize loyalty, white for purity or virtue, red for courage, yellow for hope, and green or brown for earth. In Native American culture there are four basic colors. They symbolize nature and feelings and also the four peoples of the earth: red, white, black, and yellow. Red symbolizes the sunrise of hope and the sunset of rest and thanks. White, the color of snow, is for cleanliness, purity, innocence, honesty and good intentions. Black, the color of night and in crow or raven, is for death, mourning, restoration and rebirth to the "happy hunting ground." Yellow, the color of the sun, is for the warmth and promise of "the great father."

EXERCISE 17. *Think of your favorite music, movie, book, or artwork. How were you moved by them? Can you see how what you experienced may have been due to a flash of SI, a divine spark? What can you do to improve you receptivity to an SI spark? It may help you spark more SI by going over the arts and humanities described in this chapter.*

SI SPARKS

51. Art is not an end in itself. It introduces the soul into a higher spiritual order that it expresses and in some sense explains. Music, art, and poetry attune the soul to God because they induce a kind of contact with the Creator (Thomas Merton, *No man is an island*, 1955).
52. The timelessness of art is its capacity to represent the transformation of endless becoming into being (Lewis Mumford, *The conduct of life*, 1951).

53. Great literature is simply language charged with meaning to the utmost possible degree (Ezra Pound, *ABC of reading*, 1934).

54. A little philosophy inclines the mind to atheism but depth in it brings the mind to religion (Francis Bacon, *Of atheism*, 1625).

55. The great difficulty in philosophy coming to every question with a mind fresh and unshackled by former theories, but strengthened by exercise and information (William Hazlitt, *Table talk*, 1822).

56. I believe a leaf of grass is no less than the journey-work of the stars (Walt Whitman, *Leaves of grass*, 1855).

57. Nature never did betray the heart that loved her (William Wordsworth).

58. Everyone strives to grasp what they do not know, not to grasp what they already know. Everyone knows the utility of useful things but not the utility of futility (ChuangTse, 369-280 BCE).

59. Art for art's sake is an empty phrase. Art for the sake of the true, art for the sake of the good and beautiful, that is the faith I search for (George Sand, 1804-1876).

60. The absurd is the essential concept and the first truth (Albert Camus, *Le mythe de Sisyphe*, 1942).

SI FLASHES

SI flashes are longer quotes with added opportunities to realize meditative awareness. They also are evidence from the arts and humanities for the existence of a higher consciousness or spiritual intelligence. Reflect on them to help you expand your consciousness and optimize SI.

61. 'Tis a gift to be simple, 'tis a gift to be free, 'tis a gift to come down where we ought to be; and when we find

ourselves in the place just right it will be in the garden
of love and delight. When true simplicity is gained, to
bow and to bend we will not be ashamed; to turn and
turn will be our delight 'til by 'til by turning, turning,
we come down right. (*Shaker Hymn*)

62. I am only one but still I am one.
    I cannot do everything but still I can do something
    and because I can do something and cannot do
    everything I will not refuse to do the something
    I can do. (Edward Everett Hale).

63. To look up and not down
    To look forward and not back
    To look out and not in
    And to lend a hand (Edward Everett Hale).

64. Do all the good you can by all the means you can, in
    all the ways you can, in all the places you can, at all
    the times you can, to all the people you can as long
    as ever you can. (John Wesley).

65. I would be true, for there are those who trust me;
    I would be pure, for there are those who care;
    I would be strong, for there is much to suffer;
    I would be brave, for there is much to dare.
    I would be a friend to all, the foe, the less;
    I would be giving and forget the gift;
    I would be humble, for I know my weakness;
    I would look up, and laugh, and love, and lift
    (Howard Arnold Walter).

66. I expect to pass through this world but once. Any
    good thing therefore that I can do, any kindness I
    can show to any fellow creature, let me do it now,
    let me not defer or neglect it, for I shall not pass this
    way again. (attributed to Etienne de Grellet).

67. Take the secret teaching as the bow, place on it the arrow sharp from meditation, draw it with a mind full of at-oneness. Thus arrow, target, and mind are eternal. Let OM be the bow and self the arrow, let at-oneness be the target. The target is struck through awareness, thus, arrow, target, and mind are one. (Hindu *Bhagavad Gita*).

68. All we are is the result of what we have thought; it is founded on our thoughts; it is made up of our thoughts. Speak or act with evil thought and pain follows like the wheel following the ox that pulls the cart. Speak or act with good thought and happiness follows like a shadow that never leaves you. Hate does not cease by hate at any time; hate ceases only by love. This is an Eternal Law. So, as carpenters fashion wood, the wise fashion themselves. (Buddha, *The twin verses, Sutta Pitaka*).

69. Plant a thought and reap an act;
Plant an act and reap a habit;
Plant a habit and reap a character;
Plant a character and reap a destiny
(Buddha, *Persevere, Sutta Pitaka*).

70. Though a speech be 1000 words but all senseless, one word is better that when heard brings peace; though a poem be 1000 words but all senseless, one word is better that when heard brings peace; though 1000 poems be recited but all senseless, one word is better that when heard brings peace; though a warrior defeats 1000 times 1000 others in battle, he who conquers himself is even greater (Buddha, *The 10,000s*).

71. The One God has many mystic aspects: creator and created, consumer and consumed, builder and

and destroyer beyond building and destroying, in
darkness and light yet outside both, in silence that
contains the expressed and inexpressible and sustains
all these opposites. In creation there is darkness and
light, either, both, and neither. As a child cannot
escape the mortal mother so the universe cannot
escape the Immortal Creator. God cannot be understood except by God-thinking and God-mood, hidden
and unhidden, like one seed from which all
flowers bloom. (*Svetasvatara*, Hindu *Bhagavad-Gita*).

72. Who knows for certain? Who can say? How did
creation occur? How was the universe born? Gods
came after this world's formation. Who then can know
the true origin? No one knows. Who sees it from the
heavens surely knows. Perhaps not (Hindu *Rig Veda*,
X:129).

73. To live content with small means, to seek elegance
rather than luxury, refinement rather than fashion;
to be worthy, not respectable; wealthy, not rich; to
study hard, think quietly, talk gently, act frankly; to
listen to stars and birds, to babes and sages with open
heart; to bear all cheerfully, do all bravely, await
occasion, never hurry. In a word, to let the spiritual,
unbidden and unconscious grow up through the
common. This is my symphony.
(William Henry Channing).

74. I do my thing and you do your thing. I am not in
this world to live up to your expectations and you
are not in this world to live up to mine. You are
you and I am I and if by chance we find each other
it's beautiful. If not, it can't be helped.
(F. W. "Fritz" Perls, founder of gestalt therapy)

75. Lord, make me an instrument of your peace.
    Where there is hatred let me sow love; where there is
    injury, pardon; where there is doubt, faith; where
    there is despair, hope; where there is darkness, light,
    and where there is sadness, joy.
    Divine Master, grant that I may not so much seek
    to be consoled as to console; to be understood as to
    understand; to be loved as to love, for it is in giving
    that we receive; it is in pardoning we are pardoned;
    and it is in dying we are born to eternal life.
    (attributed to St. Francis of Assisi)
76. If I speak the languages of people and angels but do
    not have love I am only as a sounding gong or crash-
    ing cymbal. If I have the gift of prophecy, understand
    all mysteries, have unlimited knowledge and faith
    that can move mountains but do not have love, I am
    nothing. If I give everything to the poor and even give
    up my life but do not have love, I gain nothing. Love is
    patient; love is kind. It does not envy; it does not boast;
    it is not proud. It is not rude, self-seeking, or easily
    angered. It keeps no record of wrongs. Love does not
    delight in evil but rejoices in truth. It always protects,
    trusts, hopes, and perseveres, and never fails.
    (*New Testament, I Corinthians* 13:1)
77. I was standing on the highest mountain and saw the
    sacred hoop of my people was one of many hoops that
    made one circle wide as daylight and starlight, and in
    the center was one mighty flowering tree sheltering all
    the children of one mother and father and I saw it was
    holy (John Neihardt, *Black Elk speaks*, 1961).

7

SPARK YOUR SI

Make the most of yourself.
That's all there is of you!
-- Ralph Waldo Emerson

Because SI is a type of intelligence and a personality trait, optimizing it is a personal achievement. It is done alone, though a support system is helpful. Sharing in group meditation can help. An environment rich with reflective elements is a plus, in a garden or a view of a peaceful scene. Without this, a room can be arranged to set a meditative mood. A relaxed, unhurried lifestyle with time for calm reflection is conducive to higher consciousness. Here are some suggestions to optimize your spiritual intelligence:

ENRICH YOUR DAILY ROUTINE

Find one item in the daily newspaper that to you shows a higher level of meditative awareness. It may be in a news story, feature article, ad, or photo. Do the same watching TV. Try to find something in your daily life more than "business as usual" that involves a higher consciousness. Find something in your daily routine that could be spiritual in some way. Developing SI is a private process so what you find inspiring may not be so to others.

CREATE A PEACEFUL PLACE

Every night, in bed ready to fall asleep, imagine your own personal peaceful place. You must be there alone or it may become a social situation. It should not be a real place. That prevents memories of times and people that would distract you. It is a place where you are always safe and feel relaxed. The place varies with the person and whatever is calming. Some choose a cabin in the woods, a hut on a beach or on a mountain, sitting in a garden, or on a boat on a calm sea.

Picture your peaceful place as you fall asleep. Take a long, slow deep breath to help you relax. Do not resist invading thoughts. Let them flow over and through you and away, like a TV commercial of no interest. Pay no attention to them. If they bother you focus on details of your peaceful place. It strengthens the imagery and weakens interrupting thoughts.

In addition to this mental peaceful place it helps to find or create a real place for calm reflection. In the outdoors, a quiet garden, park bench, or favorite place in the woods or riverbank are ideal. Indoors, a small table in the corner of the bedroom or living room help escape from the noise of everyday life to your peaceful place. Some find a candle, incense, and a restful picture or icon helpful.

TAKE MINI-VACATIONS

During the day, take a moment to briefly visit your peaceful place. Close your eyes, take a long, slow deep breath as you do so. Of course, you shouldn't do it while driving or doing anything that requires close attention. Try meal times before the first bite, at your desk just before work, on breaks, and after breaks and meals. Other times are on a bus, subway, train, or plane, after you get into or before you leave your car, and in the bathroom. The more you use it, the stronger it becomes. It can be an instant tranquilizer available to you at any time.

MEDITATE

Meditation is a unique and effective way to optimize SI. It is best done in a relaxed position. The yoga lotus position is not necessary. A stable, balanced posture is best. The object is to be comfortable but not so comfortable as to fall asleep. Fifteen to twenty minutes is a good time limit. Disconnect the phone if you can't find a place where you won't be disturbed. Lie down, on your back if in bed or on the floor, legs separated slightly, arms out from your sides, palms up, a pillow under your head. This is the "corpse pose" in asana yoga.

What is meditation like? It varies from one person to another. There are typical signs, the most common a more relaxed feeling than before. There is usually slow, shallow breathing and a loose, relaxed body. There can be eyelid flutter or muscle twitching. These are not signs of anxiety but due to nerve endings randomly firing as fine muscles relax. There are many ways to meditate but Buddhist and yogic methods are those most used.

The best way to meditate is to get into a comfortable position. The yoga lotus position is not necessary. A stable, balanced posture is best. The object is to be comfortable but not so comfortable as to fall asleep. Fifteen minutes is a good time limit. Disconnect the phone if you can't find a place where you won't be disturbed. Lie down, on your back if in bed or on the floor, legs separated slightly, arms out from your sides, palms up, a pillow under your head, the *corpse pose* in asana yoga.

A tape recorder makes a useful timer. Use one that clicks off at the end of a tape (most do). A 30-minute tape gives you 15 minutes on each side. You'll need only one side. Record the sound from a blank TV channel -- it sounds like the surf. Be sure there's no faint music or voices. This is much like "white sound," conducive to deep relaxation. If possible use it once a day at a quiet time. Lie down and start the tape, adjusted to a soft, low volume at high bass level. You have fifteen minutes of meditation to be in your peaceful place before the recorder clicks off. Don't get up right away. Linger a few minutes and enjoy the afterglow effect.

What is meditation like? It varies from one person to another. There are typical signs, the most common a more relaxed feeling than before. There is usually slow, shallow breathing and a loose, relaxed body. There can be eyelid flutter or muscle twitching. These are not signs of anxiety but due to nerve endings randomly firing as fine muscles relax. There are many ways to meditate but Buddhist and yogic methods are those most used.

Buddha' used meditation for self-mastery and to overcome the effect of a stressful world and not a cosmic consciousness as in yoga. His method can be used any time of day, best up to a half hour, in a quiet place outdoors or indoors. Born and raised Hindu, he used a basic yoga sitting position, upright, legs crossed and folded, body forming a pyramid. Hands should rest on the lap, thighs, or in a symbolic gesture (*mudra*). Meditation can be in any position, anywhere, any time, sitting (*zazen*), standing, or walking (*kinhin*). The best attitude is to expect nothing and to be patient. There is no "fast food" meditation.

Buddhist meditation can be *steady state* (*samatha-bhavana*) or *insight* type (*vipassana-bhavana*). *Steady state* is 1-pointed focus such as on a color, flame, water, or body function. Signs of it are inner calm, freedom, or rapture. *Insight* meditation aims at total absorption. If breathing is the subject, it focuses on every detail such as air before, during, and after every breath, its flow in and through nostrils, the sensations, and "becoming one with" the whole process. *Steady state* is often used to begin *insight* meditation. You can meditate with eyes open watching a peaceful scene, a picture on the wall, carpeted floor, desk top, furniture, etc..

Buddha suggested ways to prepare mentally for meditation. He said it is helpful to have loving kindness (*metta*), compassion (*karuna*), sympathetic joy (*mudita*), and non-judging mind (*upekka*). Loving kindness should be toward one's self as well as others and when correcting mistakes, yours and of others. Compassion is doing something to relieve suffering in you and others. Sympathetic joy is happily sharing in the good fortune of others and without envy or resentment. Non-judging mind is in accepting everyone and everything without bias. There are several ways to meditate, according to Buddha:

On the body. Buddha said breathing should be a close personal friend. If you didn't breathe you would die. Get to know this friend in the sensation of intake and outlet. Use silent self-talk: "I Breathe in ... I breathe out." Respect its freedom. It knows what it is doing. Experience relaxation with every breath in and out. Develop this simple awareness to appreciate this friend who is with you always. Let it help you calm yourself with its peaceful effect. This may seem strange at first but it opens the way to deeper meditation. It is like *dressage*, the way a horse and rider learn to adapt to each other.

Body meditation should be practiced daily and, at first, with silent self-talk. In the morning: "I am waking up." Walking: "I am walking." Tell yourself what you are doing as you reflect on it. With practice, meditating on breathing expands consciousness. By breathing you become one and one with all living things. Breathing out can help you let go of needless thoughts and feelings, giving them up and away to the open air, selflessly, with loving kindness. Breathing also teaches impermanence, that nothing remains the same, every breath is new, replacing all others.

Touch. You can pause at any time, anywhere, and be meditatively aware of the texture of what you touch, warm or cold, smooth or coarse, and any change touched lightly or firmly. Tell your mind what it is touching.

Sight. See into and through whatever you look at without labeling, judging, or interpreting. Let it be. Allow what you see to see you. Talking to yourself in this way helps develops meditative awareness.

Taste. The Japanese tea ceremony is a meditative experience. By eating slower and noticing smell, taste, texture, and temperature of food and drink you can do the same. Take time to fully experience different tastes: bland, tangy, spicy, sweet, bitter, sour, warm or cold.

Fragrance. Be aware and experience smells. Be aware of them, strong and faint, pleasant and unpleasant. Let them be, linger in them. How like people they are. Which would you choose to be a friend?

Objects. Be aware of their size and features. A rose is a good meditation object. Reflect on its many features: hard but yielding green stem, sharp thorns, soft petals, and a pleasant smell. It has been an object of meditation for thousands of years. It is also a symbol of life. Do you feel the thorn more than the flower? Any object can be used in this way. Use objects chosen at random. They are all parts of creation and the universe.

Emotion. A feeling can be used for meditation, pleasant or unpleasant, mixed, changing, or fixed. Reflect on how they come and go and strengthen and weaken. High SI is to be able to be one with them without doing anything to them or letting them do anything to you. It is to recognize them as old friends, and letting them pass through you of and by themselves. Let go of them and they will let go of you.

Thoughts. This is what Buddha called mindfulness and it is one of the eight steps of Buddha's 8-fold path. To be mindful is being aware of your mind as a close friend sharing your life. It is the friend you talk to as you meditate. It observes without taking action, like watching someone from a distance. Psychologist Ernest Hilgard called such a mental state "the hidden observer." Mindfulness separates trivia from the serious by being passive and reflective. In the *Book of Tao*, LaoTse described it as clearing muddy water by letting it be. It clears itself.

Buddha taught that as mindfulness improves, you can reflect on deeper thoughts such as good and absence of good, thinking and feeling (which is better?), lust and love, form and formless, simple and complex, serenity and stress, the "four sublime states" (compassion, loving kindness, altruistic joy, unbiased mind), and *five hindrances* of craving, hate, laziness, anxiety, or doubt.

Yoga in Sanskrit means *to yoke* or join with and into higher or cosmic consciousness, in mystic unity with the universe.

Yogic meditation is often 20 minutes twice a week, or every other day. Beginners benefit from daily practice   until a good level is reached. That usually takes a month. Yogis say it is better to meditate before meals since it slows digestion. Morning or late afternoon is better than night time because meditation is relaxing but doesn't really help you sleep.

Place. Create your own temple or ashram in a corner of a room or place in the room where you can put a candle, small flower vase, picture (still life, landscape, seascape) or small figure (Buddha, Jesus, Isis, or other). An ash tray or incense burner is optional. Some people find incense unpleasant. Having such a special place helps set a receptive mood for meditation. When you are away from it you can recall it as an object of meditation.

Position, posture. You do not have to get into the Lotus position. Painful positions interfere, unless you want to meditate on pain. If convenient, remove shoes and loosen tight clothing. Sit in a comfortable chair (a recliner is ideal) or on a pillow on the floor. Be a pyramid, legs crossed, hands relaxed on your thighs or lap, one atop the other palms up or partially open, knuckles touching. Another useful position is "the corpse pose" lying on your back on a carpeted floor, head on a pillow, legs parted, feet apart, arms at but slightly away from your sides, hands palms up, fingers relaxed.

Candle. Place a candle in a holder or small dish and light it. Concentrate on the flame. The outside is bright, white and yellow, inside a blue oval. Within the blue oval is a small open area of where there is no flame. The wick glows orange-red at the tip, black just beneath it, white at the candle. The candle itself is of hard wax, smooth to the touch. Where it burns it is as clear as water and runs slowly down the candle's side. What is the message of the candle? Its parts? How are *you* like a candle?

MANTRA

A *mantra* is a special word or syllable, letter or an abbreviation, chanted or visualized silently. One of the oldest and most used is *OM* or *AUM, the Sacred Syllable, The Word, Primordial Sound, Voice of Nature* or *God.* Try this experiment: Sit relaxed, mouth slightly open, no more than a half inch. Take a deep breath and make sound as you exhale without thinking of any tone. It will probably be a low tone like a moan. As you make that sound, slowly close your mouth. You've repeated the sacred syllable! It will sound like *AH-OO-MM.*

AH is beginning and creation, a call to life, breaking primordial silence. *OO* is the life force flowing through the universe, not resonating inside as the *AH* sound. *MM* is the end state, the sound of mystic unity completing the cosmic process and the mantra. You can use *OM* without sounding it aloud. You can visualize it, and in a variety of typefaces or forms. You can imagine hearing it chanted by a man, woman, a chorus, children, or your own voice. If you repeat do it slowly. Some use it for a breath inhaled or exhaled.

THE WAY OF THE WISE

Developing SI takes time. Like other intelligences, it must be used, exercised, to reach its full potential. It also takes time to develop meditative awareness. Religions differ in how they optimize SI. Thomas Merton (1968) described "the way of the wise "as "a spiritual discipline in which there is at once wisdom and method ... a journey without maps." He added that "one at times meets other travelers along the way, from other lands and traditions."

This reflects the universality of SI and implies its potential for world peace. He concluded:

> It is at the same time the highest action and the purest rest, true knowledge and selfless love, knowledge beyond knowledge in emptiness and unknowing, willing beyond will in apparent non-activity, the highest striving in the absence of striving or contention (p. 218).

It may seem contradictory that an intelligence can be optimized without factual knowledge or traditional education. It's a school without books and experiencing that is more earned by one's self than learned from books. You do not withdraw from external reality but uses as if taking an elevator to a higher floor. In Merton's words:

> It is an escape from contradiction and confusion, for it finds unity and clarity only by plunging into the very midst of contradiction, by accepting of emptiness and suffering, renunciation of passions and obsessions with which the whole world is on fire. It does not withdraw from the fire. It is in the very heart of the fire yet remains cool because it has the gentleness and humility that come from self-abandonment, hence does not seek to assert the illusion of the exterior self (p. 218).

It's difficult to optimize SI in industrialized nations. There are more distractions, busyness, and emphasis on things. As societies become more complex the risk of shaping personality to a group norm increases. In his *Professor at the breakfast table* (1860), Oliver Wendell Holmes wrote: "Society is always trying in some way or other to grind us down to a single flat surface." E. E. Cummings felt more strongly: "To be nobody-but-yourself in a world which is doing its best night and day to make you everybody else means to fight the hardest battle which any human being can fight and never stop fighting." Scottish psychiatrist R. D. Laing wrote how it feels in his book *Knots* (1970): "They are playing a game. They are playing a game at not playing a game. If I show them I see they are I shall break the rules and they will punish me. I must play their game of not seeing I see the game."

Though developing SI is a solitary pursuit there are communal aspects such as sharing in something greater than one's self and fellow feeling in one human family. With higher SI there is more acceptance and love for all people and all things, above and beyond differences. Religion gives it many names. Examples: grace, cosmic consciousness, mystic unity, the one, and nirvana. Fritz Perls, founder of gestalt therapy, wrote: "To suffer one's death and be reborn is not easy." There is a higher level of awareness, of being part of the universe and "one with it."

EXERCISE 18. *To help further develop the 16 S-traits, make a list of them for easy reference or bookmark them in Chapter 2. A personal journal is also useful. You can make brief notes of when you apply them. Reviewing your journal from time to time helps keep the S-traits fresh in mind. It reassures you of your ability to apply them. Give yourself credit for doing so. Take the Spiritual Awareness Inventory every year. Don't look at your previous year's responses until after you've taken it. That way you'll be able to see how you've optimized your SI.*

EXERCISE 19. *There are 121 SI sparks in this book. Putting an index tab at each section can help you refer to them –and enjoy them as an SI snack!*

SI SPARKS

101. Life is like peeling an onion. We peel off one layer at a time and sometimes we weep (Carl Sandburg).

102. The philosophies of one age become the absurdities of the next. The foolishness of yesterday becomes the wisdom of tomorrow (William Osler).

103. God is in me. I am in God. I want Him, I seek Him. He seeks me and we find each other (Vaclav Nijinksy, 1890-1950, his last note in his diary).

104. We tend to seek social approval on the horizontal plane rather than spiritual devotion on the vertical plane (Martin Luther King Jr.).

105. If I have been wrong in my agnosticism, when I die I'll walk up to God and say: "Sir, I made an honest mistake" (H.L. Mencken).

106. I could believe only in a God who can dance (Friedrich Nietzsche, in *Thus spake Zarathustra*, 1892).

107. The quality of mercy is not strained, it drops as the gentle rain from heaven upon the place beneath. It is twice blessed. It blesses those who give and those who receive (Shakespeare, in *Merchant of Venice*, Act IV, Scene 1, edited gender-free)

108. Live the life you've imagined (Henry David Thoreau).

109. Teach us, Lord, to serve you as you deserve, to give and not count the cost, to fight and not heed the wounds, to work and not seek rest or reward except knowing we do your will (Ignatius Loyola).

110. Do I contradict myself? Very well then, I
   contradict myself. I am large. I contain multitudes
   (Walt Whitman, *Leaves of grass*).
111. The mind of a bigot is like the pupil of the eye. The
   more light you apply, the more it contracts (Oliver
   Wendell Holmes).
112. An enthusiast broods over the oppression of a people
   till he fancies himself commissioned by Heaven to
   liberate them (Abraham Lincoln, Cooper Union
   speech, February 27, 1860).
113. It ain't the parts of the Bible I don't understand that
   bother me. It's the parts I do understand (Mark
   Twain).
114. God is the first and the last, the manifest and the
   hidden, and has full knowledge of all things (*Qu'ran*,
   Iron, 1, Cleary 1993 translation).
115. To see the earth as we now see it, small and blue
   and beautiful in that eternal silence where it floats
   is to see ourselves as riders together, brothers who
   see now they are truly brothers (Archibald MacLeish).
116. It's never too late to be what you might have been
   (George Eliot).
117. The trail is the thing, not the end of the trail. Travel
   too fast and you miss all you are traveling for (Louis
   L'Amour).
118. Keep your face to the sunshine and you won't see
   the shadows (Helen Keller).
119. God opens minds by collision and collapses of
   old local traditions, in excruciating experiences,
   to momentarily illuminate with a fuller and truer
   vision than previously possible (Arnold Toynbee,

in *Civilization on trial*, 1948).

120. From Rabindranath Tagore:
   (a) What you are you do not see. What you
       see is your shadow.
   (b) Every child comes with a message that
       God is not yet discouraged about us.
   (c) Blessed are those whose fame does not
       outshine their truth.
   (d) Bigotry tries to keep truth safe in its hand,
       with a grip that kills it.
   (e) A mind all logic is like a knife all blade.
       The hand bleeds using it.

121. Begin with certainties and end in doubt.
    Begin with doubts and end with certainties.
    (Francis Bacon, in *Advancement of learning*, 1605)

EPILOG

The world is shrinking. TV news media transmits events as they happen. Computer e-mail joins nation worldwide in one communications link. On the negative side, diseases like AIDS, SARS, and flu spread as people travel. Religious extremists spread terrorism anywhere. Muslim extremists who flew the hijacked airliners on 9/11 did so in the name of Allah against American infidels. Yet, the peoples of the world are becoming more interdependent. An early sign was the formation of the United Nations, then the European Union. Immigration in the United States shows growing Asian and Latino populations.

Like it or not, as the world shrinks everyone is in closer contact despite differences in language and culture. We know of each other and more about each other. World history shows we have not often been Good Samaritans, spiritually intelligent persons despite personal differences. Too often the nations of the world have behaved more like Cain coveting his brother's goods.

SI is a gift. What will we do with it? What will *you* do with it? Albert Einstein once said: "The future of our world is not dependent on the action of the masses so often manipulated by predatory powers and submerged in the black mire of superstition and ignorance, but on the less than 2% who have an enlightened conscience, trying to act on the facts as reason and intelligence has unfolded them, and thus they become the medium for the world's redemption."

Unknowingly (but perhaps not!), Einstein gave an estimate of those with a highly developed SI: 2%. A small minority indeed, and in a world obsessed with power and self-interest. Freeing such a world is an uphill struggle. It has always been so. Teilhard's *hominization* takes time. Perhaps that's the message in *Genesis* when Adam and Eve were forbidden to eat the fruit of the tree of knowledge. *They were not ready* to understand, realize, or appreciate that level of knowledge. Is religious extremism that condones violence another example?

SI is a universal trait and a genetic gift to the whole human race, with great potential for peace and harmony despite all the many differences of race, religion, culture, and politics. The spirituality of Moses, LaoTse, Buddha, Jesus, and Muhammad is compatible, similar though not identical. Each of them and other spiritual leaders "did it their way" but agreed love is better than hate and peace is better than war. The similarities far overshadow the differences. So, it is possible to realize a non-sectarian spirituality. SI supplements and need not supplant religion.

Gregory Bateson wrote: "The pathology of wrong thinking in which we live can only be corrected by an enormous discovery of those relations in nature that make up the beauty of nature." He saw how the nature we live in is part of our own nature: "Every discovery concerning human behavior in the external universe is also a discovery about the self."

There is good and evil in nature, in the universe, and in us. It is hoped this book will help light the way from the darker side of our nature. May it help you understand the scope and depth of spiritual intelligence and further develop it in yourself. The world is in great need of light and higher spiritual intelligence.

When Buddha was asked to define truth he said it is like a diamond of many facets. Every facet reflects some truth but only the whole diamond is truth in all its aspects. In his 1902 book *Varieties of Religious Experience,* William James wrote: "Each of us has an angle of observation, a certain sphere of fact, a syllable of human nature's total message and it takes the whole to completely spell out the meaning." It is hoped this book helps you see "the diamond of truth" in all its facets. There are higher values and a higher consciousness. From the research writing this book, and many years of life experience (I'm 81 as I write this), and nine facets of truth are clear to me:

1. Truth is sacred regardless of its source.
   There are many paths to it.
2. All life has purpose. Respect it.
3. There is good in the universe, in everyone and
   everything. Find it. Appreciate it.

4. It is better to love than hate. Make the choice.
5. All men and women are brothers and sisters. All children are their children -- one family.
6. It is better to do good and to do no harm.
7. It is better to give than receive. Grow from it.
8. Life is a mission as well as a career. Find and fulfill yourself in both.
9. Choose to be positive. Do no harm. You and the world will benefit.

These truths are not earthbound. They apply not only worldwide but throughout the universe. Sir James Jeans, the British astronomer, was asked how many stars there are like our sun and planets like earth that can sustain life. He answered: "As many as grains of sand as on all the beaches in the world." It's likely there is life on other planets. It may or may not be similar to life as we know it. There is SI there because all life forms have some level of intelligence.

The science that took us to the moon and outer space can also help us explore *inner space* and higher consciousness. To do that, science needs to process data from religion, the arts and humanities. Religion needs to open itself to the fact that not everyone will be converted to one sect. Science and religion can join in an alliance to move the world from conflict to confluence. Doing so would strengthen both, humanizing science and objectifying religion. They would arrive at higher ground together. The collaborative research on the *Dead Sea Scrolls* proves it's possible. *The truth is sacred regardless of its source.*

If the world continues as in the past, we will stand by helplessly weeping for what we are, what we are doing to each other, and what we are becoming. Sadly, only tragedy has opened eyes and hearts. Right now, at this moment, you cannot open the world's eyes and hearts but you can open your own. Abraham Lincoln once gave this advice: "Whatever you are, be a good one!" No one is perfect. Everyone makes mistakes. It's important to learn from them especially when they involve interacting with others. F. B. Meyer's "prayer" at the end of each day expresses that idea: "Father, forgive me for anything I have said or done today to cause pain to anyone. Forgive me if I have missed an opportunity to show kindness or sympathy to anyone. Help me do whatever I can to lessen sorrow and bring happiness."

Years ago, working in Alaska, I heard "the sourdough's credo." As you look back on yourself year to year, it can be an SI yardstick to help you realize how you've grown spiritually:

> **I ain't what I'm gonna be;**
> **I ain't what I wanna be; but**
> **I sure as hell ain't what I used to be!**

Whatever good has come to you from this book, share that light with others. Raise your SI finger, as Michelangelo's God and Adam on the Sistine Chapel ceiling did, toward each other -- and let the energy flow!

And from the *Star Wars* movie:
May the force be with you!

REFERENCES

Allport, G.W. (1950). *The individual and his religion.* New York: Macmillan.

Allport, G.W. (1955). *Becoming: Basic considerations For a psychology of personality.* New Haven CT: Yale University Press.

Arnold, E. (1892). *The light of Asia.* Boston MA: Roberts Brothers.

Barker, K. et al (Eds.) (1985). *The NIV Study Bible, New International Version.* Grand Rapids MI: Zondervan.

Barkow J.H., Cosmides, L., & Tooby J., (Eds.) (1992). *The adapted mind: Evolutionary psychology and the generation of culture.* Cambridge, England: Oxford University Press.

Bateson, G. (1979). *Mind and nature, a necessary unit.* New York: Dutton.

Bateson, G. (1991). *A sacred unity: Further steps to an ecology of mind.* New York: Harper Collins.

Beck, E.M. (Ed.) (1968). *Familiar quotations by John Bartlett.* Boston MA: Little, Brown and Company.

Benedict, R. (1951). *Patterns of culture.* Boston MA: Houghton Mifflin.

Bennet, E.A. (1966). *What Jung really said.* London, England: Macdonald.

Bettelheim, B. (1977). *The uses of enchantment.* New York: Vintage.

Bodhi, B. (1984). *The noble eightfold path.* Kandy, Sri Lanka: Buddhist Publication Society.

Bose, A.C. (trans.) (1966). *Hymns from the Vedas.* Bombay, India: Asia Publishing House.

Bregman, L., & Thierman, S. (1955). *First person mortal: Personal narratives of illness, dying, and grief.* New York: Paragon.

Buber, M. (1958). *I and Thou.* New York: Scribner.

Buddharakkhita, A. (trans.) (1985). *The Dhammapada, Buddha's path of wisdom.* Kandy, Sri Lanka: Buddhist Publication Society.

Campbell, J. (1976). *The hero with a thousand faces.* Princeton NJ: Princeton University Press.

Campbell, J. (1976). *Creative mythology. The Masks of God series.* New York: Viking Penguin.

Campbell, J. (1976). *Occidental mythology. The masks of God series.* New York: Viking Penguin.

Campbell, J. (1976). *Oriental mythology. The masks of God series.* New York: Viking Penguin.

Campbell, J. (1976). *Primitive Mythology. The masks of God series.* New York: Viking Penguin.

Camphausen, R.C. (1992). *The divine library.* Rochester VT: Inner Traditions International.

Cleary, T. (1993). *The essential Koran.* Edison NJ: Castle Books.

Daraul, A. (1969). *A history of secret societies.* New York: Pocket Books.

DeShazer, S. (1991). *Putting differences to work.* New York: Norton

DeWaal, F. (2006). *Our inner ape.* New York:Riverhead Trade.

Elkins, D.N., Hedstrom, L.J., Hughes, L.L., Leaf, J.A., & Saunders. C. (1988). Towards a humanistic-phenomenological spirituality: Definition, description, measurement. *Journal of Humanistic Psychology, 28,* 5-18.

Emmons, R.A. (2000). Spirituality and intelligence: Problems and prospects. *International Journal for the Psychology of Religion, 10(1),* 57-64.

Evans, R.I. (1970). *Gordon Allport: The man and his ideas.* New York: Dutton.

Festinger, L. (1957). *A theory of cognitive dissonance.* Stanford CA: Stanford University Press.

Flanagan, S. (1989). *Hildegard of Bingen.* London, England: Routledge.

Ford, M.E. (1994). A living system approach to the integration of personality and intelligence. In R.J. Sternberg & P. Ruzgis (Eds.), *Personality and intelligence.* New York: Cambridge University Press.

Fowler, J. (1981). *Stages of faith: The psychology of human development and the quest for meaning.* New York: Harper-Collins.

Fox, R.L. (1986). *Pagans and Christians.* New York: Harper and Row.

Frank, L.R. (Ed.) (1999). *Quotationary.* New York: Random House.

Freud, S. (1927). The future of an illusion. *Complete psychological works of Sigmund Freud, 21:5-36.* London, England: Hogarth Press.

Freud, S. (1933). *New introductory lectures on psychoanalysis.* New York: Norton.

Freud, S. (1949). *An outline of psychoanalysis.* New York: Norton.

Freud, S. (1953). Totem and taboo (1913). Volume 3. *Complete psychological works of Sigmund Freud,* London, England: Hogarth.

Freud, S. (1960). The psychopathology of everyday life (1901). Volume 6. *Complete psychological works of Sigmund Freud.* London, England: Hogarth.

Freud, S. (1961). *Civilization and its discontents* (1930). New York: Norton.

Fromm, E. (1951). *The forgotten language.* New York: Rinehart.

Fromm, E. (1955). *The sane society.* New York: Rinehart.

Fromm, E. (1956). *The art of loving.* New York: Harper.

Gardner, H. (1985). *The mind's new science.* New York: Basic Books.

Gardner, H. (1993). *Multiple intelligences.* New York: Basic Books.

Gardner, H. (1998). *Frames of mind.* New York: Basic Books.

Gardner, H. (1999). *Intelligence reframed.* New York: Basic Books.

Gardner, H. (2000). The case against spiritual intelligence. *International Journal for the Psychology or Religion, 10(1)*, 27-34.

Gibran, K. (1923). *The prophet.* New York: Knopf.

Gilligan, C. (1982). *In a different voice: Psychological theory and women's development.* Cambridge MA: Harvard University Press.

Gilligan, C., Hammer, Y., & Lyons, N. (1990). *Making connections.* Cambridge MA: Harvard University Press.

Goertzel, B. (1994). *Chaotic logic.* New York: Plenum.

Graves, R. (1974). *Mrs. Fisher and the future of humor.* New York: Haskell House.

Grof, S. (1984). *Ancient wisdom and modern science.* Albany NY: State University of New York.

Halevi, Z.S. (1979). *Kabbalah, tradition of hidden knowledge.* New York: Thomas and Hudson.

Hall, T.W., & Edwards, K.J. (2002). The spiritual assessment inventory: A theistic model and measure for assessing spiritual development. *Journal for the Scientific Study of religion, 41.2*, 341-357.

Hauser, M.D. (2006). *Moral minds.* New York: HarperCollins.

Hawking, S.W. (1988). *A brief history of time.* New York: Bantam.

Heidegger, M. (1963). *Being and time.* New York:

Harper Row.

Henschel, A. (1955). *God in search of man, a philosophy of Judaism.* New York: Farrar, Straus, and Cuddy.

Hick, J. (1973). *The philosophy of religion.* Englewood Cliffs NJ: Prentice-Hall.

Hill, P.C., & Hood, R.W. (Eds.) (1999). *Measures of religiosity.* Birmingham AL: Religious Education Press.

Hoge, D.R. (1972). A validated intrinsic religious motivation scale. *Journal for the Scientific Study of Religion,* 369-376.

Holy Bible, eight translation New Testament (1974). Wheaton IL: Tyndale.

Holy Bible, New Revised Standard Version (1989). Nashville TN: Thomas Nelson.

Holy Bible, 21st Century King James Version (1991). Gary SD: Deuel Enterprises.

Hood, R.W. (Ed.) (1995). *Handbook of religious experience.* Birmingham AL: Religious Education Press.

Horney, K. (1950). *Neurosis and human growth.* New York: Norton.

Hume, R.E. (trans.) (1985). *The Upanishads.* Petaluma CA: Nilgiri Press.

Huxley, A. (1963). *Literature and science.* New York: Harper and Row.

Huxley, F. (1974). *The way of the sacred.* Garden City NY: Doubleday.

Husserl, E. (1972). *Ideas: A general introduction to pure phenomenology* (1913). New York: Collier.

Ions, V. (1987). *The world's mythology of color.* Secaucus NJ: Chartwell.

James, W. (1923). *The principles of psychology* (1890). New York: Holt.

James. W. (1958). *The varieties of religious experience: A study in human nature* (1902). New York: New American Library.

Jones, R.T. (1985). *The great Reformation.* Downers Grove IL: InterVarsity Press.

Jung, C.G. (1958). *Civilization in transition.* Princeton NJ: Princeton University Press.

Jung, C.G. (1963). *Memories, dreams, and reflections.* New York: Pantheon.

Jung, C.G. (1966). *The relations between the ego and the unconscious.* Collected works, Volume 7. Princeton NJ: Princeton University Press.

Jung, C.G. (1971). *Psychological types.* Collected works, Volume 6. Princeton NJ: Princeton University Press.

Kabat-Zinn, J. (1990). *Full catastrophe living: using the wisdom of your body.* New York: Dell.

Kaplan, A. (1993). *Sepher Yetzivah.* York Beach, ME: Weiser.

Kapleau, P. (1965). *Three pillars of Zen: Teaching, practice, enlightenment.* Boston MA: Beacon Press.

King, B.J. (2007). *Evolving God.* New York: Random House.

Kohlberg, L. (1981, 1984). *Essays on moral development, Volumes 1 and 2.* New York: Harper and Row.

Laing, R.D. (1972). *The divided self.* Baltimore MD: Penguin Books.

Lamsa, G.M. (1933). *The Bible from the Aramaic Peshitta.* Philadelphia PA: Holman.

Leavens, R.F. (Ed.) (1955). *Great companions: Readings on the meaning and conduct of life from ancient and modern sources.* Boston MA: Beacon Press.

Lickona, T. (1991). *Educating for character: How our schools can teach respect and responsibility.* NewYork: Bantam.

Machlis, J. (1963). *The enjoyment of music.* New York: Norton.

MacHovec, F.J. (1972). *Yoga, guide to tranquility.* White Plains NY: Peter Pauper Press.

MacHovec, F.J. (1973). *Om, a guide to meditation.* White Plains NY: Peter Pauper Press.

MacHovec, F.J. (1979). The cult of Asklepios. *American Journal of Clinical Hypnosis, 22,* 2.

MacHovec, F.J. (1984). Current therapies in the ancient East. *American Journal of Psychotherapy, 38,* 1, 87-96.

MacHovec, F.J. (1986). The Tao of personality, therapy, and life. *Journal of Religion and Psychotherapy. 9,* 2, 75-80.

MacHovec, F.J. (1989). *Cults and personality.* Springfield IL: Charles C. Thomas.

MacHovec, F.J. (1994). Near death experiences. *Psychotherapy in Private Practice, 13,* 99-105.

MacHovec, F.J. (2005). *Light from the East: A gathering of Asian wisdom.* Berkeley CA: Stone Bridge Press.

MacHovec, F.J. (2007). *Buddha, Tao, Zen: The mystic triad.* www.lulu.com

MacHovec, F.J. (2007). *Exploring inner space: Voyage of self-discovery.* www.lulu.com

MacHovec, F.J. (2007). *Pocket Buddha.* www.lulu.com

MacHovec, F.J. (2007). *Pocket Tao.* www.lulu.com

MacHovec, F.J. (2007). *Pocket I Ching.* www.lulu.com

Maslow, A.H. (1964). *Religions, values, and peak experiences.* New York: Viking.

Maslow, A.H. (1968). *Toward a psychology of being.* New York: Van Nostrand Reinhold.

Maslow, A.H. (1969). *The psychology of science.* New York: Regnery.

Maslow, A.H. (1970). *Motivation and personality.* New York: Harper and Row.

Maslow, A.H. (1971). *The farther reaches of human nature.* New York: Viking.

Metzner, R. (1998). *The unfolding self: Varieties of transformative experiences.* Novato CA: Origin Press.

Maturana, H.R., Varela, F.J., & Uribe, R. (1974).

Autopoiesis: The organization of living systems, its characterization and model. *Biosystems, 5,* 187-196.

McCrae, R.R., and Costa, P.T., (1997). Personality trait structure as a human universal. *American Psychologist, 52,* 5, 509-516.

Mendelssohn, F. (1913). *The story of a hundred operas.* New York: Grosset and Dunlap.

Merton, T. (1967). *Mystics and Zen masters.* New York: Dell.

Merton, T. (1968). *Faith and violence.* South bend IN: University of Notre Dame Press.

Monk, R. C., Hofheintz, W.C., Lawrence, K.T., Stamey, J.D., Afflech, B., & Morowitz, H.J. (2002). *The emergence of everything: How the world became complex.* New York: Oxford University Press

Naranjo, C. (1973). *The healing journey: New approaches to consciousness.* New York: Pantheon.

Naranjo, C., & Ornstein, R.E. (1971). *On the psychology of meditation.* New York: Viking.

Newberg, A.B., and d'Aquili, E.G. (1998). The neuropsychology of spiritual experience. In H.G. Koenig (Ed.). *Handbook of religion and mental health.* San Diego CA: Academic Press.

Nisbett, R. (2002). *The geography of thought: How Asians and Westerners think differently.* New York: Free Press.

Ouspensky, P.D. (1962). *The psychology of man's possible evolution.* New York: Knopf.

Pargament, K.I. (1997). *The psychology of religion and coping,* New York: Guilford.

Peale, N.V. (1987). *The power of positive thinking.* Pawling NY: Center for Positive Thinking.

Peterson, C., and Seligman, M.E.P. (2003). Character strengths before and after September 11. *Psychological Science, 14,* 4, 381-384.

Piedmont, R.I. (1999). Does spirituality represent the sixth factor of personality? Spiritual transcendence and the five-factor model. *Journal of Personality, 67,* 965-1114.

Pribram, K.H. (Ed.). (1994). *Origins: The brain and self-organization.* Hillsdale NJ: Erlbaum.

Rogers, C.R. (1951). *Client-centered therapy.* Boston MA: Houghton Mifflin.

Rogers, C.R. (1961). *On becoming a person.* Boston MA: Houghton-Mifflin.

Rogers, C.R. (1977). *Carl Rogers on personal power: Inner strength and its revolutionary impact.* New York: Delacorte Press.

Runes, D.D. (Ed.) (1976). *Dictionary of philosophy.* Totowa NJ: Littlefield, Adams.

Sacks, H.I. (1979). The effects of spiritual exercises on the integration of the self system. *Journal for the Scientific Study of Religion, 18,* 46-50.

Sagan, C. (1979). *Broca's brain.* New York: Ballantine.

Sagan, C. (1995). *Demon haunted world: Science as a cradle in the dark.* New York: Vintage.

Saver, J.L., and Rabin, J. (1997). The neural substrates of religious experience. *Journal of Neuropsychiatry and Clinical Neuroscience, 9,* 498-510.

Scholem, G. (1974). *Kabbalah.* New York: Dorset.

Seligman, M.E.P., (2000). *Authentic happiness: Using the new positive psychology to realize your potential for lasting fulfillment.*New York: Free Press.

Seligmann, K. (1971). *Magic, spiritualism, and religion.* New York: Pantheon.

Shawardy, A. (Trans.) (1941). *Sayings of Muhammad.* London, England: Murray.

Skinner, B.F. (1971). *Beyond freedom and dignity.* New York: Knopf.

Skinner, B.F. (1974). *About behaviorism.* New York: Knopf.

Spearman, C.E. (1904). "General intelligence" objectively determined and measured. *American Journal of*

Psychology, 15, 201-293.

Starkey, M.L. (1949). *The devil in Massachusetts.* Alexandria VA: Time-Life.

Sternberg, R.J. (1990). *Metaphors of mind: Conceptions of the nature of intelligence.* New York: Cambridge University Press.

Sternberg, R.J. (1997). The concept of intelligence and ots role in lifelong learning and success. *American Psychologist, 52,* 1030-1037.

Sternberg, R.J. (2002). In search of a unified field of psychology. *American Psychological Society Observer, 15, 9,* 9-10, 49.

Tart, C. (Ed.) (1969). *Altered states of consciousness.* New York: Wiley.

Teilhard, P. de Chardin (1959). *The phenomenon of man.* New York: Harper and Brothers.

Thera, N. (1972). *The heart of Buddhist meditation.* Kandy, Sri Lanka: Buddhist Publication Society.

Tillich, P. (1963). *Christianity and the encounter of world religions.* New York: Columbia University Press.

Vermaseran, M.J. (1963). *Mithras, the secret god.* New York: Barnes and Noble.

Waley, A. (Trans.) (1938). *Analects of Confucius.* London, England: Allen and Unwin.

Walsh, R., & Shapiro, D.H. (Eds.) (1983). *Beyond health and normality.* New York: Van Nostrand Reinhold.

Watson, J.B. (1930). *Behaviorism.* New York: Norton.

Wechsler, D. (1975). Intelligence defined and undefined. *American Psychologist, 30,* 135-139.

Whitehead. A.N. (1926). *Religion in the making.* New York: Macmillan.

Williams, G.C. (1966). *Adaptation and natural selection.* Princeton NJ: Princeton University Press.

Wilson, C. (1971). *The occult: A history.* New York: Random House.

Wittgenstein, L. (1963). *Philosophical investigations*. Oxford, England: Basil Blackwell.

World Council of Churches (1991). *Confessing the one faith*. Faith and Order Paper. Geneva, Switzerland: WCC Publications.

Yamamori, T. (1998). *Exploring religious meaning*. Upper Saddle River NJ: Prentice Hall.

Zweig, C., & Abrams, J. (Eds.) (1991). *Meeting the shadow*. New York: Jeremy Tarcher.

More books by Frank MacHovec
www.lulu.com

Light from the East, a gathering of Asian wisdom

Buddha, Tao, Zen: Mystic triad

Exploring inner space, voyage of self-discovery

What's funny? The psychology of humor

Syzygy, a unified personality theory

Cults and terrorism

Lead and manage: The four cornerstones

Pocket I Ching

Pocket Buddha

Pocket Tao

INDEX

www.ingramcontent.com/pod-product-compliance
Lightning Source LLC
La Vergne TN
LVHW011227080426
835509LV00005B/370